Soccer Bugs

by

Bo Rush

Earth's Future Publishing

Dedicated to The Bookies, the first bookstore

ISBN 978-0-9644101-1-4

Published by Earth's Future Publishing

CONTENTS

Soccer Bugs

-1-
Stabbed!

I'm not a killer! But for as long as I can remember, there's been blood on my hands… dog blood!

Ever since I heard about the awful death of Fido Lincoln.

Most people know the story of Abraham Lincoln. How he came from a dirt-poor family and ended up being the 16th President of the United States of America. And how, after winning the Civil War and ending slavery, Honest Abe was shot dead in a theater. It's in every history book.

But the history books don't tell the whole story. You see, Honest Abe wasn't the only Lincoln family member who was assassinated!

Only a couple months after the President was shot in Washington, D.C., Fido Lincoln got killed right in broad daylight in Springfield, Illinois!

Fido was the Lincoln family pet, and a real friendly dog. He was a yellow mixed-breed who wandered all over Springfield back when it was a small town.

When Abe went to his law office to work on a case, or to the barbershop for a trim, Fido waited patiently on the sidewalk outside. When there was mail, Abe and Fido would pick it up at the town post office. Fido even helped carry packages home when Abe went to the general store.

Bottom line, Fido Lincoln was a happy, lovable, playful, and helpful dog. The Lincoln family loved him, and so did everyone that met him.

Maybe if he hadn't been so lovable, I wouldn't feel so awful.

Charlie Planck hadn't ever met Fido. He was sitting on a curb in Springfield one summer afternoon in 1865, carving a stick with a sharp knife.

Fido came bounding down the unpaved street in a happy mood. In his usual friendly way, he sprang forward with his muddy fore paws raised to say hello.

Charlie Planck was looking down as he worked on the stick. He didn't even know Fido was approaching until the dog jumped up on him.

Startled, Charlie Planck jerked back. When he spun around to see who or what was on him, the knife went straight into Fido's chest!

I live in New Abe, Illinois, which is a small

town just up the Sangamon River from Springfield. But that's not the main reason I know about Fido Lincoln.

The main reason is that my name is Rio Planck. That's right… Planck!

Charlie Planck is my great-great-great-great grandfather! That's why poor Fido's blood is on my hands!

Even though I'm ten years old and the only things I've ever killed are about a million mosquitoes and some fire ants, I feel like I'm partly responsible for the death of Fido Lincoln.

No one knows for sure whether my great-great-great-great grandfather accidentally killed Fido or did it on purpose. Either way, I don't feel any less guilty.

Last year, my third grade class went on a field trip to the graveyard in Springfield where Abraham Lincoln is buried. We found out his body is kept in a real actual tomb – not in a regular grave like everyone else in the cemetery!

It was a pretty good field trip, but I would have liked it a lot better if we'd had time to go to Fido's grave, too.

I owe that dog a big apology!

-2-
Three True Facts

True Fact #1: Troy Niles is the best player on my soccer team. He might even be the best youth soccer player in all of Sangamon County.

True Fact #2: Troy Niles is also a world-class jerk who always seems to ruin my life.

Last year, Troy was the scoring leader and MVP as the Springfield Matrix went undefeated. We won the Central Illinois League championship with a perfect 8-0 record.

Being a member of a title team is great – even when you didn't have much to do with all the victories. I'm a decent midfielder, but on the Matrix I'm pretty much a nobody – at least I was last season.

This year, I'm planning on playing a bigger role. I know it won't be easy. The team's loaded with big-time scorers, tough defenders, and the best goalkeeper in the league.

But I've been practicing non-stop since last year. We play against the fifth-graders everyday at recess. I go one-on-one with Pike the Slobberer in our backyard. And Grandpa Dan has shown me a bunch of new moves and drills.

That's why I showed up thirty minutes early to our first practice of the season. I used that time to squeeze in one final workout. When the rest of the team arrived, I was sweating like a pig.

Mr. Niles, Troy's father, is the coach. He's also the district manager of a company that sells soybeans in five states that border Illinois. It's impossible to forget that fact because bigmouth Troy brags about it all the time.

Like anyone cares about soybeans... or district managers… or fathers…

To get things started, Mr. Niles called all the players together. I noticed right away a couple new kids on the team. They were either clones or identical twins. They were both tall – even taller than Troy – with thick chests, muscular arms, and huge square heads. These two probably could've grown mustaches if they wanted.

Although I'd never seen them before, it seemed like the twins already were best buddies with Troy.

"First things first," Mr. Niles began, "we have some business to take care of. A whole lot of extra kids signed up to play soccer this year," he nodded toward the clones standing on either side of Troy. "In fact, so many kids signed up, the league decided to start a whole new team."

"Does that mean we get to play extra games?" someone asked.

"No, the number of games will be the same," explained Mr. Niles. "What it *does* mean is that two of you will switch over and play on the new team."

Man, how bad would that be? Get cut from the best team in the league and have to go play with a bunch of rejects!

The fairest thing would be if the two new kids – the identical twins – transferred to the new team. But since they looked super athletic and were probably soccer all-stars, I knew they were safe.

You see, Mr. Niles loves winning even more than he loves soybeans. He'd for sure keep the clones and cut the two worst players on the team. No way he'd let someone go who might help the Springfield Matrix win another title.

I looked around at the other faces, wondering who the unlucky pair might be. The other kids were doing the same thing.

"The two who will be switching teams are…" Mr. Niles looked down at a notecard and cleared his throat. "Aurora Woodstock…"

That was no big surprise. Aurora was a weak defender who practically screamed and ran the other way whenever the ball came near.

Everyone stared at Aurora like she'd just died or something. Surprisingly, she didn't look all that disappointed. She just smiled and fingered her rainbow headband. Maybe she thought it was a special honor to get cut from the team!

"And, let's see…" Mr. Niles looked again at the notecard.

The other reject would probably be Elgin Cooper or Sonora Morton. They were both benchwarmers last year, with little hope of cracking the Matrix starting lineup this season.

My guess was Elgin because one of his legs is longer than the other one. I felt sorry for him and Aurora, but at least they'd get a lot more playing time on a losing team.

"Rio Planck."

My head snapped back. For a second, I didn't know who'd said my name. When I realized it was Mr. Niles, I thought maybe he wanted me to do something – like get a bag of soccer balls out of his jeep.

But, that wasn't it! That wasn't it at all! No… NO!… NO!!

I desperately wanted to tell Mr. Niles how hard I've been practicing since last year and how much I've improved! But there was a gigantic lump stuck in my throat that was making it hard to swallow.

"Aurora and Rio, you two report to Lincoln Park tomorrow at 4:30 for your new team's first practice."

All the kids on the team stared at me like they were waiting for me to make a farewell speech or something.

I was paralyzed, suddenly sick to my stomach. A black cloud swirled around me and the ground kind of shifted under my feet.

"What's the name of our team?" Aurora asked brightly.

"I don't think they have a name yet," Mr. Niles chuckled.

I might've felt a little better if all the Matrix players had come over to bump fists and tell us how much they'd miss us. But they didn't.

Instead, they acted like Aurora and I had a deadly disease that they didn't want to catch.

Mr. Niles blew his whistle and ordered the team to form two lines for passing drills.

As everyone ran off to start practice, I stood there and tried to figure out what had just happened.

"It might be fun to join a brand new team," Aurora continued to be positive.

That's when it hit me. I knew why I had been cut from the Matrix – and it had nothing to do with my soccer abilities!

It was all because I dared to laugh at Troy Niles at recess!

Troy and the other fifth grade soccer stars were beating us fourth-graders like they do every day. They don't just beat us – they destroy us! They pulverize us until there's nothing left of the entire fourth grade class except a thin sliver of toe jam!

And it's 99.9% due to the incredible talent of Mr. MVP – Troy Niles. He'd be the first to tell you.

I have to admit, Troy *is* a gifted soccer player. The ball seems to be magically attached to his feet, and his long legs eat up the soccer field. He cuts through the fourth grade defense like the Sangamon River flowing through the willow trees that stretch from here to Decatur.

Last week at lunch recess, I chased after Troy on a breakaway. Even though I'm probably the fastest runner in fourth grade, I couldn't make up any ground on him.

As Troy sped toward the goal, he swung his powerful right leg to shoot at the near post.

"Dwight! Watch out for the fake!" I yelled to our goalkeeper.

Too late! Dwight went for the fake, diving at

the right post. The left side of the goal was so wide open, Troy could've scored with two broken legs and a dislocated belly button!

But… just as he was about to send the ball into the net, a dark blur came out of nowhere, cutting in front of him!

Troy's right foot swung forward, but it hit nothing but air. The momentum spun him around. He lost his balance, fell backwards, and skidded on his bottom right across the goal line!

Watching Mr. MVP slide butt-first into the goal was one of the funniest things I'd ever seen! But I kept my mouth clenched shut. I knew if I cracked the tiniest grin, Troy would instantly vaporize me. That's the kind of epic jerk he is.

I was able to lock my lips for a second or two, but then it just exploded out of me.

"Great butt-goal, Troy!" I chirped between laughs.

Troy's face instantly twisted into a hate-filled death stare. I knew I should get ready for his all-out attack, but I couldn't stop laughing!

To my surprise, Troy turned away from me. "Stop her!" he yelled. "Stop Radiohead!" He jumped to his feet and took off after the ball thief.

Whoa! Talk about dodging a major bullet!

I turned and watched the dark blur suddenly transform into a long-legged girl. Two stiff black braids stuck out on either side of her head as she zoomed away with the soccer ball. She was running so fast, I was surprised I didn't see smoke coming from her heels!

The fourth and fifth graders charged at the ball thief from all directions – but she dodged left and right between them all!

I don't remember ever seeing anyone run so fast that they actually turned into a blur! That girl was running like her backside was on fire!

She cranked her right leg and drilled the ball into the opposite goal. She kicked it with such incredible force, I half expected to see the ball explode right through the back of the net!

"Wow! Great shot!" I called to the girl as she sped away across the playground.

Troy spun angrily toward me. I guess I didn't dodge his bullet after all.

"You'll be sorry you said that, Planck!" he threatened.

"Said what?" I shot back. I knew I should keep my mouth shut, but whenever Troy bullies me, I turn it into a big joke. I can't resist it.

"You know what!" he growled.

"All I said was *Wow! Great shot!* Or do you mean…" I hesitated, a mischievous smile forming on my lips. "*Great butt-goal*!"

Troy spit, swore, and stepped toward me.

My hands automatically balled up into fists, even though I knew they'd be useless against his lethal assault.

Troy came right up to me and stopped. I could smell the bean burrito he'd eaten for lunch on his breath.

"It *was* a great butt-goal, Troy! It was probably the best butt-goal in the history of soccer!"

I would've kept talking, but a cruel smile began to curl on Troy's thin lips. I knew exactly what that signaled – his final assault!

He let me squirm for a few seconds, before finishing me off.

"Fido!" Troy spat out in a mean, mocking voice.

Even though he didn't lay a finger on me, it felt like he'd driven his fist right into my stomach.

I tried to block that dead dog from my mind, but Troy began barking.

And I was destroyed… just like that.

That's how Troy always wins our little battles. He calls me *Fido,* and I'm instantly reduced to rubble.

Mr. MVP laughed triumphantly and strutted away like he'd won some big gold medal.

I just stood there, rubbing my hands against my jeans, trying desperately to wipe off Fido

Lincoln's blood.

Aurora climbed into her mom's minivan, and I walked over to my bike. Behind me, I could hear the exciting sounds of soccer practice. That's when I felt the full impact of the awful thing that had just happened.

I hopped on the bike and pedaled furiously. I wanted to get away from the park as fast as possible – before anyone saw the tears suddenly streaking down my face.

True Fact #3: Mr. Soybean was the one who cut me from the Springfield Matrix – but his rotten son handed him the knife.

-3-

The Ultra Rejects

I wasn't expecting to find a lineup of incredible soccer talent when I arrived at my new team's first practice. However, what greeted me there was way beyond my worst fears.

Gathered on the field at Lincoln Park had to be… the sorriest collection of soccer players ever assembled on one team!

Most of the kids I knew from school and from playing in the Central Illinois League. Aurora Woodstock, of course, was there with her rainbow headband and matching knee-high socks.

Mitchie Wheaton spun around in a circle and laughed crazily as he crashed to the ground. Mitchie's actually a pretty fast runner. The problem is, whenever he kicks a soccer ball, it flies off in totally random directions – usually straight up!

I spotted Fulton Harvey. Fulton's a fifth-grader, but he's such a tortoise that Troy Niles makes him play on the fourth grade team at recess. What's worse, Fulton is the kind of kid who always wears hundred-dollar vapor-grip goalie gloves, even though he almost never plays goalkeeper.

Then there was Cary Moline. Cary's a pretty easy-going guy, but he can be really hard headed about some things – like running. You see, Cary doesn't run. I mean, *never*. He refuses. He doesn't even like to walk very fast. It doesn't matter what's going on – a soccer game, relay races, a fire drill… Cary trudges, end of story.

Alton Huntley played for Decatur last year. Well, he didn't actually play much – at least, not soccer. Alton mostly stood on the sideline and messed around with his phone. Apparently, not much has changed – I saw his phone inches from his nose.

I was surprised to see Dawson Downs and Sterling Sandoval. They're in my class at New Abe Elementary, and I know for a fact that neither girl has ever played on a soccer team before. Not even at recess. They must've signed up because all the spots on the hula hoop team had been taken.

Put together, these seven players possessed less soccer skill than what Troy Niles had in his left pinkie toe.

As I gazed at my new teammates, I slowly realized something… We weren't just a team of ordinary rejects. We were *way* beyond that. We're talking… *ultra* rejects!

Other teams would destroy us! The Matrix would probably set a world record for the most lopsided victory ever! The soccer field scoreboard would overheat and explode trying to keep up with all the Matrix goals!

If I'd been a quitter, I would've turned my bike around and gotten out of there as fast as possible! This team was destined to lose and lose big, maybe even set some world records for being terrible.

But something kept me from leaving. It was one of Grandpa Dan's sayings…

"If you're gonna take the trouble to do something, it's foolish not to give it your best shot."

I always try to be positive about things, a glass half full kind of guy – even when I don't feel that way on the inside.

So… I adjusted my shin guards and headed off to join my new teammates.

"Hiya, Mitchie!"

"Dude!" Mitchie dizzily held out his knuckles and tried to bump mine.

"Hey, Aurora," I waved.

Aurora smiled dreamily as she ran her fingers around her rainbow headband.

I gave the other kids a friendly nod and thumbs up, trying to be a good teammate and act confident about our chances, despite the grim reality.

That's when I spotted the blur girl – the one Troy Niles called Radiohead. She stood quietly to the side and a little behind the others.

She'd just moved to New Abe from Chicago, so I didn't know much about her. But I'd seen how fast she could run and how hard she could kick. Maybe she and I could team up and put enough shots in the net to actually beat somebody.

Some bald-headed guy I'd never seen before told us to gather around him. I knew he wasn't our coach because he didn't have a bag of soccer balls.

"I'm Mr. Cobden from the Central Illinois League Youth Soccer Association. How are you guys doing today?"

He gave us an awkward smile. A few of the other kids said, "Hi," but I was wondering what bad news this guy had for us.

"We're still looking for a coach for you guys," the bald-headed guy continued. "Hopefully, we'll have someone in place by next week. If any of your parents would like to volunteer, I'd be happy to talk to them."

"My dad would volunteer, except he works at the manure warehouse over in Pekin," said Alton.

"My brother might do it," said Dawson, "but

he lives in Oregon."

"You can talk to my ma," joked Mitchie, "but she doesn't know anything about soccer."

A bunch of other kids raised their hands and offered various family members and pets, but I stopped listening.

I already knew who would be the perfect coach!

-4-
Grandpa Dan

The red and white checkerboard New Abe Taxi was parked in its usual spot in front of our house, so I rode my bike around back. This time of year, I knew he'd be in the garden.

"Grandpa Dan! Grandpa Dan!"

I couldn't wait to tell him! I knew he'd be super psyched about my idea!

Grandpa Dan's mastiff met me as I entered the backyard. He jumped up with his front fore paws and slobbered all over my face – his usual greeting.

"Hey, Pike!" I hit the brakes and gave him a big hug.

I spotted Grandpa Dan in the garden. Even though he was kneeling down and half hidden by all the plants, his red and white checkerboard baseball cap and vest stood out in the green jungle.

"Grandpa Dan!"

He looked up and grinned when I fishtailed to a sudden stop. "Where's the fire, son?"

There wasn't any fire. That was just Grandpa Dan's way of saying I seemed to be in a big hurry.

"You know how I told you I got stuck on a new soccer team?"

"I recall you mentioning it a time or three."

"Well, guess what?! The team needs a coach! So, I volunteered you!"

Grandpa Dan grinned. "That's a good one!" He chuckled and continued digging with a little hand shovel around some tomato plants.

"I'm not joking!" I squatted down beside him. "It'll be great!"

Grandpa Dan didn't say anything. He just kept digging in the dirt.

"Hello…?" I gently tugged on the gray ponytail that fell between his shoulders. "Grandpa Dan…?"

He ignored me. He does that sometimes, but usually it's just him joking.

"You're perfect for the job! And I already told them you'd do it!"

Grandpa Dan laughed again. "Yep! I'm perfect! Except for one little detail… The fact that I've never coached a soccer team in my life!"

I thought Grandpa Dan would be honored that I'd volunteered him to coach – and that he'd agree right off the bat. This was the last thing I expected!

"You'd be great at it, Grandpa Dan! Better than Mitchie's mom, that's for sure! You taught me everything I know about soccer!"

Grandpa Dan stabbed the little shovel straight down into the dirt and turned to me.

"It's one thing to know how to play the game, Rio. I don't know the first thing about being a coach."

"You just teach us what you know! That's all any coach does! Please, Grandpa Dan! You'd like all the kids!"

"It's not the kids I'm worried about. It's their parents! They do more shouting and screaming at those soccer games than a roomful of newborn babies!"

Grandpa Dan chuckled and started digging again in the garden.

"The parents won't yell at you! They'd all really like you!"

That last part was totally true. Everybody loves Grandpa Dan because he jokes around all the time. That's one of the main reasons I wanted him to be our coach!

Grandpa Dan stopped digging again. This time he had a real serious look on his face. It was almost sad looking.

"Look, son, I'm 62 years old."

"That's young these days!"

"Plus, I'm the owner and operator of New Abe's premier and only taxi."

"If you get a call for a ride, we'll just stop practice and wait till you get back!"

"I also have a half-acre garden that's ready to go to seed if I don't give it my undivided attention."

"I'll help you with the garden! Here… hand me that digger thing!"

Grandpa Dan sighed and scratched Pike's neck the same way he always scratches his scraggly beard.

"You ever hear a crazier idea, Pike, ol' boy?"

Grandpa Dan named every dog he ever owned Pike. That's because Pike was the nickname of his older brother who was a soldier and died way before I was born.

"Me…? A soccer coach…? Hah!"

I'd known Grandpa Dan long enough to suspect there was still a sliver of hope. If he'd just said no, that would have been the end of the discussion. But the way he was putting up such a big fight meant there was still a chance he was bluffing.

"Won't you at least think about it?" I pleaded.

"I don't need to think about it, son. The idea of me coaching a soccer team is completely idiotic, ridiculous, and laughable!"

Even though it sure didn't sound like Grandpa Dan was bluffing, I thought I noticed a mischievous twinkle dancing in the corner of his eye.

"Which is why this crazy coaching idea... sounds more fun than a forest full of lightning bugs!"

"You mean, you'll do it?!" I exploded with excitement. "You'll be our coach?!"

Grandpa Dan nodded. The grin on his face was almost as big as the one on mine!

-5-
Ghost Train

Quincy Morrison is the polar opposite of Troy Niles. He's not a world-class jerk. He doesn't brag about his soybean-loving dad. And he never bullies anyone.

In fact, Quincy's different than pretty much every kid in New Abe – even me. Which is kind of weird since we're best friends.

For one thing, Quincy's real smart. Not that other kids aren't – but Quincy is mega-mega intelligent.

His head is jammed with knowledge because he spends most of his time researching stuff. I'm talking hour after hour. Q has this crazy superhuman ability to focus on things. But only when it's a topic he's interested in.

Like hummingbirds or infrared radio waves or Antarctica.

Another way we're different is that I love soccer and play it all the time, but Quincy has zero interest in sports. I mean, none! Zippo! Zilch! Nil! Nada!

But probably the biggest difference is that Quincy has a hard time connecting with other kids.

As a matter of fact, I'm pretty much his only friend.

You see, even though Quincy is super smart, he has autism.

I'm not sure exactly what that means, but my mom's a nurse and she said Quincy's brain just works differently.

I think that's why I like him so much. He's definitely the most interesting kid I've ever met.

Quincy and I have a tradition. Every year when the weather starts to warm up in April, we go camping.

I don't mean driving far away somewhere and pitching a tent next to a bunch of other tents.

I mean sleeping in the backyard – alone. No grown-ups anywhere around, except inside in the house.

We started the tradition last year in my backyard. Grandpa Dan let us borrow his pup tent, and Quincy and I had sleeping bags and a flashlight. Pike was out there, too!

We almost made it through the whole night. But somewhere around three in the morning, we were both suddenly wide-awake.

There was lightning and thunder – and rain everywhere! It poured so hard, the tent flooded in seconds!

Pike disappeared into the house with the

first thunderclap. Quincy and I really wanted to stick it out, but we didn't have a choice. My mom showed up with an umbrella and made us go inside for the rest of the night.

This year we decided to camp in the Morrison's backyard. Mr. Morrison set up a huge zippered tent with mesh pouches hanging from the inside walls and screened windows in the ceiling.

"Hey, Q, we gotta do this every year!"

"Yeah, every year," Quincy repeated.

I rolled back and forth on top of my sleeping bag. Even though we didn't have air mattresses, it was plenty comfortable.

"Wow… Your yard is super cushy!"

"That's because my dad fertilizes the grass with compost."

"Nice…" I suddenly stopped rolling and sat up on my elbows. "Hey, uh, compost… that's not like cow pies, is it?"

"Compost is decomposed food," Quincy explained. "Food so rotten it isn't even food anymore. It's just gooey mush."

"Doesn't it really stink?"

"Yeah. It's the best substance for growing plant life in soil."

I sniffed the air. "I don't smell anything. How come it isn't stinky now?"

"The soil absorbs the odor."

“Lucky for us!” I laughed and stretched out again. I tried to forget about compost and stink.

“I know another tradition we can start,” Quincy blurted out.

“Yeah? What?”

“The ghost train.”

“Ghost train?” I sat up again. “What’s the ghost train?”

“The Lincoln Special. The funeral train that brought President Abraham Lincoln’s dead body back from Washington to Springfield.”

“Whoa! Really?”

It sounded like a great tradition so far!

Quincy continued, “The train arrived in Springfield on May 3rd, 1865. Every year since then, the funeral ghost train makes the same cross-country trip!”

“Hey! May 3rd is next week!” I said excitedly. “What do we have to do? How do we see it?”

“All we do is go to the railroad bridge over the Sangamon River.”

“Okay…” That oily black bridge has always scared me, but I’d go there as long as I wasn’t alone.

“At midnight.”

“Whoa! It has to be at midnight?” I didn’t want to go anymore, but I didn’t want to tell

Quincy that. “I don’t think our parents will let us.”

“Why not?” Quincy asked with a totally straight face.

“Because it’s at midnight. And we’re ten.”

“Oh,” Quincy answered flatly.

“We’ll have to wait till we’re sixteen and have a car and can do whatever we want!” I suggested. I figured I wouldn’t be scared of much of anything when I was sixteen.

“Okay,” Quincy agreed.

I bumped Quincy’s fist, then laid down on the sleeping bag once more.

“So… what exactly happens at the railroad bridge at midnight?”

“Lincoln’s funeral train… the ghost train… crosses the bridge.”

“Wow!”

Quincy continued, “Clouds hide the moon, and an eerie train headlight suddenly appears in the night. Clocks stop running when the train passes by. But everything’s completely silent. It’s like the train is running on a carpeted track.”

“No way!”

If any other kid had told that story, I wouldn’t have believed it for a minute. But with Quincy, it probably was true.

“Skeletons dressed in blue stand at attention next to President Lincoln’s casket. Flags attached to the train whip in the wind, but still no sound can be heard. Then, just as suddenly as it appeared, the funeral train crosses the bridge and disappears."

"Hey, Q! I don't think I can wait till I'm sixteen!"

I don't know if it was hearing about the ghost train or what, but I sure couldn't sleep very well that night.

Plus, there's one thing about Quincy that I really don't like. He snores. Loud! Like a chainsaw that needs oil! I don't know how Q doesn't wake himself up, it's so deafening!

Which was why I was lying there – on the compost grass – wide-awake in the middle of the night.

Even though everything was pitch black outside, I swear I could see the walls of the tent being sucked in every time Quincy snored in a breath. Then the tent flapped like ten tornados when he snored the air back out.

I pulled my head down deeper inside the sleeping bag. I kept thinking about that railroad bridge and wondering why it scared me so much.

I mean, one of my favorite things to do is stand next to the Sangamon and spit into the Atlantic Ocean!

Spit has your DNA in it. And everyone on

the planet has a unique DNA code, just like a fingerprint. So, it's kind of amazing to think I can spit a little bit of myself into a river in New Abe, Illinois, and it'll float away and away – twisting down the Sangamon… flowing into the Illinois River… then into the mighty Mississippi… all the way down hundreds of miles to the Gulf of Mexico, which is part of the Atlantic Ocean!

I've never been to the Atlantic Ocean, but my spit is floating around in that faraway saltwater! Who knows? My DNA might be swimming in the English Channel or washing up on the white sand beaches of West Africa!

I was awake in that sleeping bag for what seemed like hours. I was surprised it wasn't getting light out yet.

The whole time, I kept wondering if there was any way Mom would let me go to the railroad bridge at midnight.

Or if there was some other way we could see that ghost train!

-6-
Hubba-hubba!

Nine soccer balls were lined up along the penalty box chalk line.

Grandpa Dan stood next to the goal. "Let's get this show on the road! Give it a boot!" he instructed. "One at a time!"

Aurora Woodstock stepped up to the first ball. Her aim wasn't bad, but she kicked the ball with such a total lack of force that it rolled to a stop six feet in front of the goal.

Grandpa Dan clapped his hands enthusiastically. "You got the right idea, kiddo!" he shouted. "Next time put a little more mustard on it!"

Fulton Harvey gave his ball a mighty kick. But it missed the goal and nearly took off Grandpa Dan's head.

"I surrender!" Grandpa Dan dropped to his knees and waved a white handkerchief.

Dawson Downs totally missed the ball when she swung her right foot.

"Golfers call that a practice swing," said Grandpa Dan. "Now try again, kiddo. And be sure to keep your eye on that spotted orb!"

Dawson concentrated real hard on the soccer ball. But when she swung her leg, she missed again.

"That's only strike two!" Grandpa Dan called. "The odds are stacked in your favor now!"

"I'll never be able to do this!" Dawson stomped her foot and accidentally kicked the ball. It rolled straight into the net.

"Yippee!" Grandpa Dan jumped into the air. "We just avoided a shut-out!"

Cary Moline and Alton Huntley both missed the goal by wide margins. Sterling Sandoval's kick went straight up into the air. We all ducked as it plummeted back to earth.

"No worries! Rome wasn't built in a day!" Grandpa Dan piped.

There were only three ultra rejects left – Mitchie Wheaton, me, and that blur girl from Chicago.

"Go for it, Mitchie! Give it a big boot!" Grandpa Dan knew Mitchie's name because we did a science fair project together.

It was supposed to be all about Bigfoot, but the teacher in charge of the science fair said Bigfoot didn't exist, so our three-sided display board wasn't actually science.

Maybe not, but we had a whole bunch of kids crowded around our table the entire day!

Mitchie has a pretty strong leg. I know because he plays soccer with the rest of us every day at recess. He just has to work on his aim.

Mitchie gave the ball a mighty boot, but his shot sailed at least twenty feet over the goal. When Mitchie slumped his shoulders in defeat, Grandpa Dan changed that in a hurry.

"Wish I had the speed gun on that laser!"

In case you haven't noticed, Grandpa Dan tries to see the positive in just about everything.

So, that left me and blur girl. I was next in line, but thought maybe she should go first.

"You want to go?" I was surprised how soft my voice sounded.

She didn't say anything. She just took a step and sent a rocket into the back of the net.

Grandpa Dan was truly impressed. So were all the ultra rejects.

"Hubba-hubba!" Grandpa Dan crowed as he did a little dance around the goal post. "We've got our striker!"

The blur girl stepped back so I'd have enough room to kick.

For some strange reason, I started feeling nervous. That girl was a tough act to follow!

I looked down at my soccer ball, but I kept seeing her shot explode off her foot and into the net.

I blinked a couple times, trying to get the ball back into focus. I really wanted to blast it, so I swung my leg extra hard.

I don't know exactly what happened. But my right foot somehow missed the ball! I mean… it was a complete whiff! Worse than Dawson's!

The momentum spun me around, and I fell – flat on my bottom! I sat there on the grass looking like a complete fool. All I could think to say was, "Whoops…"

Everyone went silent. For the first time all practice, Grandpa Dan was speechless.

That is, until he started laughing. He slapped his knee and held his gut and howled so loud, everyone started joining in.

I looked up and saw blur girl holding her hand out to me. She wasn't laughing like everyone else.

She took my hand and pulled me to my feet. Man, she was way stronger than she looked!

"That's only strike one." She nodded at the ball, reminding me to try again.

This time, I didn't stop to think about being nervous. I didn't think about anything. I just gave the ball an angry kick. It sailed into the back of the net. Not bad… although it didn't break the sound barrier like blur girl's rocket.

That quieted everyone down. Now, I only

felt half embarrassed.

"Good shot, Rio."

I think I flinched when blur girl said my name. I'm not sure why. Maybe because I'd never talked to her in my life.

"Thanks, Radio–"

I didn't want to call her what Troy Niles called her… Radiohead.

"What's your, uh…?" I was going to ask what her name was, but I couldn't quite get the question out.

"Savanna," she answered. "Savanna Dixon."

I could tell this Chicago girl was friendly, so it was natural to be friendly right back. "Your shot was about ten times better."

"No way!" she protested. "I didn't get all of the ball."

"Yeah, well, you got way more of it than I did!" I held out my fist and she bumped it with hers.

Although we spent most of the practice running and sweating, everyone was in a real good mood – thanks to Grandpa Dan's fun-loving attitude. Even Cary Moline started to speed-walk all over the field!

Grandpa Dan ended practice by calling us together in a circle. He sat in the grass at the head of the circle.

"There's only one little fly left in the ointment." Grandpa Dan gazed around at all the kids' faces. "Who can guess what I'm referring to?"

I knew none of the kids had any idea what he was talking about. But, I knew! Grandpa Dan meant there was one more little problem we had to fix.

"Our moniker!" Grandpa Dan announced. He glanced around at the bewildered faces.

Moniker?... Even I was stumped this time.

"A name for our team," Savanna explained matter-of-factly.

"Bingo!" Grandpa Dan exclaimed as he stretched over to give her a high five.

I was sitting next to Savanna. When she turned to high five Grandpa Dan, I could see the back of her head.

Something that looked like a hearing aid was hooked behind her left ear. A thin cable connected the device to a small plastic circle stuck to the side of her head just behind her ear.

She had the same thing behind her right ear!

When she turned back toward the circle, I quickly looked away so she wouldn't know I was staring.

"Rio here's been grumbling and groaning

for the past week! He keeps talking about a team called the Ultra Rejects!"

I felt everyone's eyes on me. Sometimes I really wished I could put a cork in Grandpa Dan's mouth!

"The New Abe Ultra Rejects… That's no name for a fantastic team like this!" Grandpa Dan exclaimed. ""Now… who's got a moniker we can proudly hang our hats on?"

"How about the Robins?" offered Aurora.

"The New Abe Robins! That has a nice ring to it!" Grandpa Dan smiled. "Every year we eagerly await Mr. Robin's announcement that spring has arrived! Unfortunately, robins are nothing but pests that prey upon their young!"

Aurora recoiled in horror.

"Just teasing, kiddo!" Grandpa Dan laughed and gave Aurora a high five. "Robins are sweet, adorable creatures who will NEVER win a soccer match so long as they live."

Aurora couldn't help but smile. By now, the kids were starting to get comfortable with Grandpa Dan's sense of humor. More and more of them started cracking up at his comments.

"I've got one… The New Abe Torpedoes!" chirped Alton.

"Yes!" Grandpa Dan jumped to his feet and fist-bumped Alton.

"The Torpedoes! They destroy everything in their path! Every opponent is obliterated!" Just as Grandpa Dan was working himself into a fever, he suddenly remembered something.

"But there's one tiny little problem, son... Torpedoes blow themselves up in the process! That won't do. A winning soccer team needs staying power!"

"Oh, yeah... I never thought of the blowing itself up part," shrugged Alton.

"I know – the Waffle Cones!" laughed Sterling.

"That's actually not bad!" said Dawson as she high fived Sterling.

"Cones, for short!" added Fulton.

"I love waffle cones!" grinned Cary, licking his lips.

When the laughs died down, I decided to tell them the name that had been stuck in my head for the past two days.

"I've got one," I offered quietly.

"Not the Ultra Rejects!" insisted Mitchie. Everyone else joined in, shouting down the Ultra Rejects.

"No, this one's way better," I promised. "Well, maybe not better, but more... unique."

Everyone waited for me to let the cat out of the bag. They were suddenly so quiet I could hear the Sangamon lapping on the riverbank next to Lincoln Park.

"Well?..." Cary finally said in an exaggerated way.

"You guys have to promise not to laugh," I grinned.

"We promise!" several kids shouted.

"Okay, then… here it is…" I hesitated.

"Tell us!" everyone ordered.

"Okay, uh…"

The name stuck in my head was so unique, I wasn't sure it would go over with these nine harsh critics.

"Spit it out, dude!" Mitchie ordered.

I hesitated for a moment – thought about forgetting the whole thing.

"Lightning Bugs!" I suddenly blurted out.

I expected to be greeted with howls of laughter, but they surprised me. No one made a sound. It was as if they were all holding their breath.

After a few seconds, I heard a soft giggle… followed by another… and another… Then, like a bottled-up volcano, the whole team erupted!

They laughed so hysterically, they were practically choking. Kids rolled around on the grass trying to keep their guts from exploding!

They were laughing so hard, even I started

cracking up.

The Lightning Bugs!... Don't ask me how I ever thought of such a stupid name!

The only one who wasn't laughing was Grandpa Dan. He just sat there quietly, scratching his beard like he always does when he's thinking hard.

All of a sudden, he snapped his fingers. "By golly, it's a perfect moniker! Lightning Bugs are magical and mysterious... and everyone loves 'em!"

To my shock, all the kids quickly agreed with Grandpa Dan. I didn't know if it was because they truly liked the name or if they just liked Grandpa Dan so much. He has that effect on people.

Either way, I was starting to feel kind of proud to be a member of the New Abe Lightning Bugs!

-7-
Down in Texas

"That's the worst name ever!" Mom hooted with laughter as she tossed a leafy salad in a big wooden bowl.

"That's sorta why I like it, Marissa!" Grandpa Dan said as he sliced some carrots for the salad.

I sat at the kitchen table next to him. I'd already finished chopping up the cucumbers.

"But *The Lightning Bugs*!… Was Big Eyed Caterpillars already taken?"

Grandpa Dan chuckled at that one, which I knew would only egg her on.

"Couldn't you have come up with something a bit more aggressive sounding?" Mom asked. "I mean, it's a soccer team, not a toddler play group!"

"Lightning bugs are unique." My explanation sounded lame before it was even out of my mouth. I guess maybe I was feeling a tad defensive since the name was my idea.

"They are unique, *mijo*. You're right about that." She was trying to keep a straight face, but not doing a very good job of it.

Mom calls me *mijo* when she's feeling good.

It means "my son" and it's pronounced *mee-ho* because "I" sounds like "E" and "J" sounds like "H" in Spanish. Don't ask me why.

My mom can speak Spanish because she moved to the U.S. from El Salvador, which is a tiny country in Central America that I've never been to.

But I want to go! Mom says everyone's completely crazy about soccer in El Salvador! Plus, I've got cousins and uncles and stuff who I've never met!

"If it has to be an insect name, how about the Giant Japanese Hornets?" Mom looked totally serious, but when she glanced over at Grandpa Dan, I knew what was coming next.

I'd seen it plenty of times before.

"Or the Parasitic Worms…" Grandpa Dan volunteered.

"Vampire Moths!" Mom shot back.

"Spittle Bugs!" Grandpa Dan snickered.

I just sat back and relaxed. I knew there was nothing I could do to stop those two once the jokes started rolling.

"Stink Bugs!"

"Biting Bed Bugs!" Grandpa Dan answered.

"Hopping Mad Horseflies!"

"Maggot-infested Maggots!"

I didn't take any offense about them poking

fun at our team's new moniker. Why should I? Other than the fact that it was my pathetic little brainstorm.

"Pretty Pink Katydids!"

"No, she didn't!"

I didn't take offense because whenever Mom joined Grandpa Dan in a round of back and forth jokes, I knew she was in a good mood.

Grandpa Dan always seems to be in a good mood, but not Mom. That's because she's on her feet all day working as an ER nurse. ER means emergency room, and you can't sit down when you're busy trying to take care of a never-ending line of really sick, bleeding and vomiting people.

Plus, she has to deal with me. Not that I'm the worst kid in town or anything, but I'm a kid. Kids do stuff. Sometimes dumb stuff. And my dad's not around to help her.

Grandpa Dan does a lot for Mom and me. But it's not like he's my dad.

Actually, he *is* like my dad. More than my dad is. That's because my father is Joe Planck and he lives with his new family down in Texas. He got married again after Mom and him split up.

I'm not exactly sure why Mom and him couldn't stay married. If they'd asked my opinion, I would've voted for us staying together as a family.

It doesn't bother me that much. I guess because I haven't even seen Joe Planck in almost seven years. To be honest, I don't remember much of anything about him – other than some stuff Mom has told me.

I figure, if I did see Joe Planck again, I'd probably be disappointed. I mean, comparing him to Grandpa Dan.

It's like Joe Planck is my real father, but Grandpa Dan is my real dad.

One thing I know for sure. My father down in Texas has Charlie Planck's murderous blood inside him! Just like I do…

Which is the main reason I try not to think about him too much.

Mom placed the salad bowl in the middle of the table. She brushed a strand of hair off her face and took our hands to give thanks.

I know I'll always be thankful that Mom was the one who got custody of me after the divorce. No way I'd want to live with Joe Planck and his new family down in Texas.

-8-
Fun Time

The New Abe Lightning Bugs had three more practices before the first game of the season. Grandpa Dan had our tongues hanging out most of the time, but nobody complained.

That's because we were having so much fun! And there was one main reason why…

Troy Niles' dad was the kind of coach who never had any fun at practice. Just the opposite. He was strict and mean, and got mad at you if you messed up a pass or a shot.

He yelled at everybody – except his MVP son. I guess that's how Troy learned to be so mean to me and just about everyone else.

The only time Grandpa Dan ever hollered at Lightning Bugs practices was when he was cheering for one of his players.

"That's it, kiddo! Great job, son! Put your heart into everything you do and you'll be rewarded!" he'd yell and give a big thumb's up.

Grandpa Dan never even came close to getting mad when someone messed up at practice. He told us that mistakes are good because that's how you learn. He said if you're always afraid to make a mistake, your body gets so tense, it's like you become paralyzed!

Instead, just... put your heart into it and you'll be rewarded!

When Dawson kicked air instead of the ball, or Mitchie's shot went straight up into the clouds, Grandpa Dan would always clap his hands and shout encouragement.

"Nice try, kiddo! You can't make an omelet without breaking some eggs!"

And when someone actually made a great play, Grandpa Dan would sing out, "Hubba-hubba!!" and start doing some crazy, made-up dance.

When I was on the Matrix, I always thought it must've been weird for Troy to have the coach be someone he had to live with. But, with Grandpa Dan, it wasn't weird at all. In fact, it was great!

When all the kids on the team started calling him *Grandpa Dan* instead of *Coach*, I felt proud. Plus, Grandpa Dan and I got to talk all about the Lightning Bugs when we were eating breakfast and dinner. We discussed strategies and plays and everything! And every day the two of us (and Pike the Slobberer) had extra practice in the backyard.

Best of all, Grandpa Dan let me have a say in what the starting lineup should be!

I wrote out a bunch of lineups, but there was

one I believed gave the Bugs the best chance.

Forward:	*Savanna Dixon*
Forward:	*Mitchie Wheaton*
Winger:	*Alton Huntley*
Winger:	*Fulton Harvey*
Center Mid:	*Rio Planck*
Defender:	*Sterling Sandoval*
Defender:	*Aurora Woodstock*
Keeper:	*Cary Moline*
Sub:	*Dawson Downs*

Grandpa Dan just looked at the names, lifted his cap and scratched his head, and kind of frowned. I don't think he had any idea who was who. He just called all the girls *kiddo* and all the boys *son*.

I guess it must be really hard to learn a bunch of new kids' names.

Lightning Bugs practices were ninety non-stop minutes of races, drills, and scrimmages. But none of the kids ever begged out. That's because we were all having so much fun! Grandpa Dan even got Cary to run for the first time ever!

Most kids would agree that wind sprints are okay if you only have to do a couple of them. But if you have one of those coaches who makes you run wind sprints over and over, it turns to torture.

Lightning Bugs wind sprints were way better than normal because Grandpa Dan ran right along with all the kids. He'd start huffing and puffing and grunting and groaning so loud, we'd all collapse with laughter before we got to the finish line – and he'd win!

Grandpa Dan was fun like that throughout the whole practice. When one of the players showed any kind of improvement, Grandpa Dan dropped to his knees and bowed down like a servant before his ruler.

"Hubba-hubba! Eight straight kicks without a miss! That's a new world record, kiddo!"

If anyone began to fade out and lose focus, Grandpa Dan would redirect their attention by suddenly stating some odd and amazing fact about anything under the sun.

"Do you kids realize that the Earth is our spaceship and we're all spiraling through the universe? Pretty fun stuff, huh?"

Dribble-and-shoot drills became target practice – with Grandpa Dan as the dancing target!

At first, the other Bugs just stared at Grandpa Dan blankly when he'd start joking and dancing. But it wasn't long before the kids started laughing right along and joining him in his crazy celebrations!

Somebody would make a perfect pass or tackle and… We'd start whooping and bouncing up and down, dancing crazily and kicking out our legs like complete oddballs.

"Hubba-hubba!" became the team's rallying cry.

If Troy and the rest of the Matrix players had spotted us partying like that on the soccer field, they would have thought we were completely deranged!

Sometimes I wondered if all that joking around and having fun was a waste of valuable practice time. After all, the rest of the Central Illinois League teams were no doubt getting real serious and intense, since the season openers were right around the corner.

I try to be optimistic, but deep down I knew that a bunch of ultra rejects like the Bugs were going to lose plenty of games. Maybe every one!

Still, I didn't want to get completely humiliated on the soccer field – especially when we had to play the Matrix.

Unfortunately, that nightmarish thought seemed completely unavoidable.

"Triangle time!" Grandpa Dan called out.

No one knew what that meant. We just stood around and watched as Grandpa Dan spread us out. He positioned us ten yards apart, in a series of connected triangles.

Savanna, Mitchie, and I formed one triangle. When I made a quarter turn, Mitchie, Dawson, and I formed a different triangle. Each direction I turned, I was in a triangle with two teammates.

It was the same for all the others, except the ones along the edge.

"Now everyone start moving down the field." Grandpa Dan rolled a ball toward me. "Pass the ball around your triangle, Rio. Then advance it to the next triangle."

I booted the ball to Savanna, who one-timed it over to Mitchie. When he kicked it back to me to complete the triangle, I turned and sent the ball to Dawson.

She passed it back to Mitchie to complete that triangle, so he turned and kicked the ball to Alton to start the next one.

"Triangles are cool!" crowed Fulton.

"They're the strongest shape known to mankind!" Grandpa Dan added, as he watched our imperfect triangles move up and down the field. "A guy down in Carbondale named Bucky Fuller proved it. He even lived in a triangle house!"

"What are we building, Grandpa Dan?" joked Mitchie.

"An offense!" Grandpa Dan answered. "The triangle is the key to every successful offense!

When you have possession of the ball and you're in a triangle, you always have at least two teammates you can pass to!"

For the next twenty minutes, we passed the ball around and between the triangles. After that, Grandpa Dan showed us how to leave our spots and race over and form new triangles after we made a pass.

Before long, the soccer ball was whipping from Bug to Bug. New triangles formed faster and faster. I could see how a defense would have a tough time taking the ball away from us!

Of course, to win any matches, we had to do more than just advance the ball and play keep-away. We had to score.

Fortunately, whenever I saw how hard and accurately Savanna could kick, I couldn't help but feel hopeful. With me playing center mid and Savanna at striker, we were sure to put some shots into the net! Maybe enough to win some games!

If not… Would the New Abe Lightning Bugs be the worst team in the history of the Central Illinois League?

Or would Grandpa Dan's triangle magic transform the Bugs into a well-oiled soccer machine?

I really had no clue.

-9-
The Bridge

The railroad bridge over the Sangamon River must be a hundred years old or more. It was probably built way back when Abe Lincoln was living around here.

The wooden bridge is real rickety and super creaky. I'm kind of surprised the whole thing hasn't collapsed right into the river.

I've heard kids brag that they've walked all the way across the railroad bridge on a dare. I've never seen anyone do it, so I don't know if it's true.

All I know is, that's a dare I'll never take. Not even when I'm sixteen.

I mean, if a freight train suddenly came, you'd have two choices – get flattened by a 200-ton locomotive or jump off the bridge into the Sangamon!

Most people would jump into the river and try to swim out of the deep part, but I don't know how to swim. That's why you won't catch me walking on that spooky old bridge… ever!

We were sitting at the dinner table when I decided to bring up the idea of going to the railroad bridge to see the ghost train.

"Quincy told me about something extremely educational that he wants me to do with him," I began.

"What's that?' asked Mom.

"Watch Abraham Lincoln's funeral train on its way to Springfield."

"I've heard of that!" Grandpa Dan exclaimed. "It's supposed to be a ghost train!"

Mom didn't immediately answer, so I added, "At the railroad bridge… this Friday night!"

Mom frowned, but instead of answering, she said, "You know, President Lincoln had a dream that he was going to be killed."

"Three days before it happened!" added Grandpa Dan.

"Then why did he go to that theater?" I wondered.

Grandpa Dan took off his cap and scratched his head. "Guess you'd have to ask him." Then he grinned. "Next time you see him!"

Talking about Abe made me think of another important member of the Lincoln family.

"I wonder if Fido had any dreams about dying?" I asked to no one in particular.

"Dogs can dream," Grandpa Dan said. "I know Pike dreams. Don't ya, boy?" Grandpa Dan leaned over and squeezed Pike's slobbery muzzle in his two hands. "I've seen him grin when he's sleeping!"

"Poor Fido probably cried his eyes out during his dreams," I mourned.

"Now, don't start torturing yourself about that dog," Mom laughed as she gathered up the dirty plates.

"But he was stabbed by a Planck!" I reminded her.

"That happened a hundred and fifty years before you were born, son!" Grandpa Dan chuckled.

"So?! What do you two know, anyway! *You're not Plancks*!"

Then I glared at Mom and said something I regretted even before the words came out of my mouth. "Except by a marriage that didn't last!"

Everyone went quiet. The only sound was Mom setting the stack of plates in the sink.

My eyes went straight down to the floor. I was too embarrassed to look at either of them at the moment.

When I finally snuck a peek, Mom didn't look mad at all. Instead, she kind of smiled gently.

"I'd love to take you and Quincy to see the ghost train, Rio. I really would! But I have to work an early shift on Saturday."

I nodded and said softly, "That's okay,

Mom."

I really didn't care about going to that bridge anymore. I was too relieved that Mom wasn't hurt by what I'd said. At least, she didn't look hurt.

Mom just messed with my hair and kissed my forehead. Then she started loading the plates into the dishwasher.

Since she wasn't ticked off, I decided to try once more. "Q and I could ride our bikes out there…" I said it real casually, hoping my suggestion wouldn't seem totally outrageous. "…at midnight."

Mom turned toward me. "Oh, you could, could you?" She was still smiling, but now it wasn't so gentle. It was more like I'd just told a not-so-funny joke.

"Uh, yeah."

"The two of you…"

"Yeah."

"At midnight…" She obviously wasn't crazy about the idea.

"Well, it's not like anything bad would happen." I said it, but even I was having a tough time keeping a straight face.

"Of course, not!" Mom completely agreed. "What could *possibly* go wrong at the railroad bridge at midnight?"

I was ninety-nine percent sure she was being

sarcastic, but there was still that one percent.

"So… is that a yes?"

"Why, of course it is!"

Mom turned on the dishwasher, dried her hands on a little hand towel hanging from the refrigerator door handle, then rearranged a pair of El Salvadoran candleholders on the windowsill.

I sat there and waited. I knew she wasn't done answering my question.

She spoke to me over her shoulder as she left the kitchen. "When you're eighteen."

Oh, well… It had been a long shot. At least for a few moments it took my mind off that mean ugly thing I'd said to Mom.

"I'll take you boys!" Grandpa Dan suddenly piped up. "We can go in the taxi! If that's okay with you, Marissa."

I looked over at Grandpa Dan and he gave me a wink. My thumb shot up in victory.

Mom poked her head back in the doorway.

"Sounds like a whole lot of fun, Marissa!"

Mom didn't immediately answer. She bit her lip like she always does when she's deciding something.

"Please, Mom! It'll be totally safe with Grandpa Dan!"

If it had been some ordinary grown-up, like Quincy's dad, Mom wouldn't have thought twice about it. But Grandpa Dan wasn't remotely close to ordinary.

Mom always jokes that he's just a big gray-haired kid. Maybe so, but that's what makes it so much fun to be around Grandpa Dan!

"I'm sorry about what I said before," I added in a guilty voice. "And I'm not saying that just to get you to agree."

That last part was actually true. One of the really dumb things I do is get mad and say some mean thing to Mom that I instantly regret.

Sometimes she gets mad right back. Mom may be a nurse who helps people all the time, but that doesn't mean she doesn't have a temper. Believe me, I've seen it in action!

But usually she doesn't get mad. She just does what she did today – be kind and loving. In a way, that's worse because then I feel even guiltier.

So, I've learned to just own up and apologize right away. It's way better for everyone.

Grandpa Dan checked his phone and pushed back his chair. "Some fella over in Blue Mound needs a lift." As he got up to go, he gave me a parting wink. "Let me know the final verdict."

As Grandpa Dan went down the stairs to his room in the basement, Mom sat back down in her chair. The sarcastic smile was gone. In its place was… well, just Mom… Marissa Cordova… Her brown eyes had a real honest look – kind of weary, a little sad, but loving at the same time.

"It's natural for you to be angry that your parents got divorced."

I looked down. She always says something logical like that. But logic isn't always the answer.

"I'm angry about it, too," she added.

I looked up in surprise. "You are?"

She nodded. "A tiny bit. Not so much anymore."

"But, you used to be? You were *really* mad at him?"

"I was mad at both of us. Mad… and disappointed… and heartbroken." She paused and wiped a tear from her eye.

"Yeah…" my voice was barely more than a hollow croak. "Me, too."

Mom reached out and put her hands on mine. I didn't want her to be sad, not even a little bit.

"You know what, Mom?" I said, trying my best to lift her spirits.

"What, *mijo*?"

"It's only a tiny bit for me, too – just like you!" It was actually more than a tiny bit, but I don't like it when she worries about things.

Mom smiled and squeezed my hands. "Time heals…" she said softly.

I knew what that meant – little by little, the terrible pain goes away as the years pass.

"I love you, Mom."

"I love you, *mijo*."

I couldn't resist asking again. "So… about Friday…"

Mom laughed loudly. "Were you just playing with me?"

I nodded and grinned – even though we both knew I meant every word.

She was still laughing as she picked one of my dirty soccer socks off the floor.

"Hey! I've been looking everywhere for that!"

I reached out for the sock, but she held it away.

"Why was it wedged under the fridge? Why isn't it in the laundry?"

"I *put* it in the laundry! It must've somehow gotten out!" I didn't even try to keep a straight face for that one. "Wait! It was probably Pike! Is it covered in slobber?"

Mom sighed in exasperation. "You're ten, Rio. You need to do it right – and *then* some. Who do you think picks up my dirty clothes?"

"One of your personal minions?"

Even though I thought that was a pretty funny thing to say, I could tell by the beady eye

Mom gave me that she didn't.

"Okay, we'll make a deal," she announced. "You can go to the bridge on Friday – if *this* disgusting thing is in the laundry in five seconds!"

Before I could agree to the deal, Mom dropped the sock onto the floor.

"*Uno*!"

I leaped out of my chair and scooped up the dirty sock. As I veered for the laundry room, Mom jumped in my path.

"*Dos*!"

"No fair!" I dodged around her and flew down the back hallway. Truth is… I like any kind of challenge – even a silly one like this.

"*Tres*!"

I burst through the laundry room door and dove for the wicker laundry basket.

"*Cuatro*!"

Right arm fully extended, I slam-dunked the sock into the dirty laundry – just as Mom called out, "*Cinco*!"

Which is how, on a moonless Friday night – as clocks all over Illinois ticked toward midnight – Quincy and I sat in stony silence in the backseat of the New Abe Taxi. The only lights we could see were a few faint glimmerings coming from New Abe farther down the river.

If it had been just Quincy and me alone out here, I'd be too jumpity to enjoy the adventure. But sitting in the taxi with Grandpa Dan made everything seem totally safe.

The taxicab was parked on a lonely gravel road that runs alongside the Sangamon River. Just ahead, I could barely make out the tall outline of that spooky old railroad bridge.

Thick woods lined both sides of the river. Thousands of lightning bugs flashed on and off in the trees.

"They put on quite a show, don't they?" Grandpa Dan remarked. "I once found a frog that lit up like a light bulb from eating so many lightning bugs."

"That's so incredible!" Quincy exclaimed.

With Grandpa Dan, you never knew for sure exactly how much of what he said was fact and how much was fiction. But it was so much fun to listen to him that it didn't matter.

"Did I ever tell you boys about the time I got tapped on the shoulder by a ghost?" Grandpa Dan said in a secretive voice as he turned toward us.

I'd heard the story before, but I shook my head because I knew Quincy would get a bang out of it.

"It was real late… the deadest part of night… three A.M. I was out cold, sleeping like a log. I was dreaming about something or other, when a finger – a single lone index finger – reached out and tapped me! Twice, right on the shoulder. The tap felt so real, I woke right up. But nothing was there, so I figured I was just dreaming and went back to sleep."

I looked over at Quincy. His eyes were open wide.

"Two weeks later, middle of the night, the same thing happened. The finger tapped me twice on the shoulder! I jerked awake and swung my arm out to touch whatever was there. I flipped the lights on, but – nothing!"

"Wow!..." Quincy whispered.

"Naturally, I was wondering what the blazes was going on. The finger taps had been firm, like someone was trying to wake me up. But who?... And why?... Then, two weeks after that, I got tapped a third time! I jumped straight out of my skin and hit the light switch! My heart was pounding a mile a minute. I couldn't see anything unusual in the room, but that didn't matter. I knew something was there! So I just stood next to the bed and waited. 'C'mon! I'm right here!' I called out. For two hours I stood there like a statue. I couldn't do anything else. There's no way I could go back to sleep.

"What happened then?" I could tell Quincy

was dying to find out.

Grandpa Dan shrugged. "That's what's really strange. Nothing happened. Nothing at all. The finger never came back. Although I slept with a light on for about the next six months."

"Mom says bad luck always comes in threes." I'm not sure why I said that.

"I'm not so sure it was bad luck," Grandpa Dan replied. "Maybe I was being warned about something. Maybe it was trying to wake me up to some kind of danger."

"Did anything bad happen to you after that?" asked Quincy.

"Nope, nothing. I moved in with Rio and his ma. That was probably bad luck for them!" Grandpa Dan chuckled.

As midnight ticked closer, our voices hushed. The screeching of a million crickets filled my ears. I stared out the window at the night. It was intensely dark – like a living, breathing black cloud.

"The Lincoln Special comes from the north," Quincy whispered, nodding toward the far side of the black river.

I cocked my ear and tried to listen for the ghost train, but remembered that it moves silently.

"Only one more minute!" Grandpa Dan nodded at the dashboard time display… 11:59!

Quincy and I sat upright in the back seat. I don't think I even breathed for the next sixty seconds.

After what seemed like an hour, the time display suddenly flipped to 12:00!

I peered into the darkness, trying to catch a glimpse of the ghost train.

"There she is!" Grandpa Dan leaned forward and pointed.

Quincy and I dove into the front seat. Our wide eyes scanned the darkness for a train headlight.

"I don't see it!" I said anxiously.

"Me either!" added Quincy.

Grandpa Dan kept pointing. "Right over there! Coming through the trees!"

Quincy and I both pressed closer to the windshield, straining to see the train's single headlight in the blackness.

"Wait! I think she stopped!" Grandpa Dan squinted hard. "Yep! She's stopped over there in the woods on the other side of the river!"

The car door swung open and Grandpa Dan hopped out.

"Hand me that bag, Rio!"

He pointed to a small duffle bag on the floorboard by the gas pedal.

I picked up the bag and handed it to him.

"Where're you going, Grandpa Dan?!"

"Across that bridge to find out what the blazes is going on!"

"But, Grandpa Dan—!"

"You two stay put!"

Just like that, Grandpa Dan disappeared into the darkness! The last thing I saw was him reaching into the duffle bag as he headed toward the bridge.

"What's in that bag?!" Quincy shuddered. "Maybe he has a knife!"

I could tell Quincy was as scared as I was.

"Or a gun!" he shuddered.

I tried to catch a glimpse of Grandpa Dan, but he had completely vanished!

"What if a train comes across that bridge when he's on it?!" I cried. "Does the ghost train ever stop like that?"

"No. It just appears and disap–"

"Shh–!" I shushed and stuck my head out the open window.

It sounded like there was some kind of struggle on the bridge!

"Help–!" someone cried out. It sounded like Grandpa Dan's voice!

Quincy went stiff as a board next to me.

A second later, we heard a loud splash in the river!

Then… silence. Dead silence. Even the crickets were suddenly mute.

I fell back into the seat. My heart was pounding against my chest and I wasn't sure how much longer I could breathe.

What if something bad had happened to Grandpa Dan?!

"You think he's…?" Quincy was thinking the same thing.

"I don't know!" I snapped.

I wasn't yelling at Quincy, but I didn't know what to do! Get help… or hide… or…

Suddenly, I threw open the driver's door and vaulted out of the taxi! "Come on, Quincy! We've got to find him!"

I looked back over my shoulder – Quincy hadn't budged. It looked like he was sinking deeper into the seat.

"Staying here… staying here… staying here… staying here…" he repeated over and over. That's what Quincy does when he gets nervous.

"Not a problem, Q…" I tried to calm him. "You stay here."

"Staying here… staying here…"

I knew Q might completely freak out if I left him alone, but I didn't have a choice. There wasn't a second to waste!

"Don't leave till I get back!"

I quickly turned and headed for the railroad bridge. Its wooden outline loomed like a giant guillotine against the midnight sky.

"Grandpa D-Dan?..." I called out in a trembling voice.

An owl hooted, its eerie call echoing over the black river.

My eyes darted in every direction as I approached the bridge. All I could see were shadows and darkness.

"Grandpa Dan!"

I took another step – and tripped! I fell forward onto oily wooden ties beneath the two steel rails.

Frantically, I scrambled to my feet and tried to regain my bearing. I was standing on the railroad track – one step away from the bridge!

I looked over the side railing and glimpsed the deep waters of the Sangamon rushing far below.

What if I have to rescue Grandpa Dan from the river?!... How am I gonna do that?!... I can't even swim!

Cupping my hands to my mouth, I called out in desperation. "Grandpa Dan!... Grandpa Dan!"

I cocked an ear and listened as hard as I could. Again, there was no answer – just the lonely calls of birds and screeching insects.

The far end of the bridge disappeared into the black night. Grandpa Dan had to be over there!

Gulping hard, I squinted at the tracks. Nothing was coming… No train or stranger or—!

"Ahh--!" A half-choked scream filled my throat as someone grabbed my arm! I swung around to face the attacker.

"Q…!"

"St-st-stick together!" blurted Quincy.

He had a death-grip on my arm. But I didn't care! I'd never been so happy to see him!

"Stick together… Stick together… Stick together…"

Even in the darkness I could tell Quincy's face was pale as a ghost.

"Calm down, Q. Everything's okay," I told him, even though I knew it was just the opposite.

"Stick together… stick together…"

A sudden warm gust of wind swept over us, making the wooden bridge creak and moan.

"Grandpa Dan said he was going across." I looked toward the far end of the bridge.

Quincy's fingers dug deeper into my arm. His teeth chattered like hailstones hitting a metal barn roof. "Stick together… stick together…"

I peered into the black night… Still no light from a train. "Grandpa Dan!" I called out once more.

Again, nothing… nothing but the creaking bridge and the terrible total darkness.

My knees were shaking – shaking so badly, I didn't know if I was standing on my own or if Quincy was holding me up!

"We have to c-cross the b-b-bridge…" My voice shook even worse than my knees. I was trying to convince myself as much as convince Quincy.

I took a deep breath, then began inching across the bridge, stepping carefully from tie to tie. My eyes jumped back and forth from the railroad tracks to the silent black waters far below.

If Grandpa Dan fell off the bridge, the river current would've carried him away by now! But he knows how to swim! He's a good swim–

"Rio–!" Quincy screamed, nearly ripping my arm off.

I looked up into the blackness and was immediately blinded! A single bright headlight was coming right at us!

Quincy and I froze like statues as the light rushed closer! It wasn't making a sound!

It had to be the ghost train!

"Run!" I yelled, grabbing Quincy's hand.

We both turned and ran as fast as we could back the way we'd come from! I leaped over two ties at a time all the way to the end of the bridge, then dove to the ground to the side of the tracks!

But Quincy tripped stepping off the bridge and lost his balance!

I reached out and grabbed him just before he face-planted on the tracks! As I stood him up, I glanced up.

The headlight was still coming! Except it wasn't a train headlight! It was bouncing up and down like someone was carrying it!

"Four score and seven years ago…"

We froze again. It was… President Lincoln's voice!

"Our fathers brought forth on this continent a new nation…"

My eyes bugged open wider and wider. A tall stovepipe hat poked up behind a blinding flashlight!

Abraham Lincoln! Coming right at us!

"This is so incredible!" Quincy squealed in disbelief.

"Conceived in liberty and…"

I recognized that speech! It was one of his most famous ones! The Gettysburg Address!

But I didn't care about that. There was something else I was dying to know! "Why'd you go to that theater if you knew that guy was going to shoot you?"

"Dedicated to the proposition..."

I was a little surprised that Abe wasn't taller. I'd always heard that he was the tallest president.

"That all men are created equal and…"

Wait a second! There was something awfully familiar about President Lincoln's voice…

"The Lightning Bugs shall win their first game tomorrow!"

"Why, you—!" I grabbed the flashlight from Abe's hand and shined it in his face.

Grandpa Dan took off the stovepipe hat and grinned. "I guess Old Abe was right! You *can* fool all the people some of the time!"

I didn't know whether to hug Grandpa Dan for being alive or kill him for pranking us!

I hugged him… But I made sure to squeeze extra tight just so he'd know I wasn't totally happy!

-10-
On the Nose

Honest Abe might've been our country's greatest president, but he was wrong about the Bugs defeating the Decatur Dynamite in the season opener. Dead wrong.

In the first half, Grandpa Dan tried a trio of goalkeepers, but none could keep Decatur's shots out of our goal.

Cary Moline didn't even come close to laying a finger on Decatur's first three shots of the game. We were behind 3-0 after four minutes!

Fulton Harvey subbed in for Cary, but the Dynamite scored three more goals during his stint. Actually, they only kicked in two, but Fulton accidentally punted one backwards into our goal.

Aurora Woodstock was more of a spectator than a goalkeeper. Decatur tallied four more goals before the half came to a merciful end.

On offense, the Bugs tried to use the triangle formation to move the ball. But it only seemed to work when Savanna Dixon was one of the triangle's corners. She blasted in two goals to keep us from being totally humiliated.

I'm pretty good at counting, but I still had to look at the scoreboard to see exactly how bad the halftime score was… 10-2.

Ten goals given up in one half! The Matrix didn't allow ten goals all last season!

The other Lightning Bugs collapsed on the grass around Grandpa Dan. I wasn't sure if they were exhausted from all the running or depressed by the lop-sided score. Probably both.

I couldn't sit. I was too sick to my stomach. All I wanted to do was get back out there and turn this turkey around!

"What a first half of soccer you Bugs played! Each and every one of you! Amazing!"

We were getting beat like a drum, and Grandpa Dan made it sound like we'd just won the World Cup.

"By golly, you make me proud to be your coach!"

No one said anything, or even looked the least bit hopeful. Not even Grandpa Dan's infectious enthusiasm could lift this team's sunken spirits. Forget all that fun we'd been having at practice. Getting massacred by Decatur ruined it all.

When I closed my eyes, I could see the whole soccer season quickly going down the drain. Another half as miserable as the first one, and some of the kids on the team will call it quits – guaranteed! We might not even have enough players next week to fill out a starting lineup!

When the referee blew his whistle to get the two teams back on the field for the second half, I looked around at all the others. It was obvious that most – if not all – of my teammates had already thrown in the towel!

Cary rolled over onto his stomach and buried his face in the grass. Alton stared longingly at the cell phone sticking out of Grandpa Dan's vest pocket. Sterling and Dawson looked at their parents like they were hoping they would come and taken them far, far away.

Even Savanna didn't look ready and willing.

Grandpa Dan motioned for us to huddle up on the sideline. "Trailing ten to two is nothing!"

Of course, everyone knew that was a lie.

"All we gotta do is score nine times and blank 'em the rest of the way!" he continued enthusiastically. "Then we'll cook up some good ol' Decatur goose!"

He looked around at the circle of uncertain faces. No one looked the slightest bit convinced.

"Like my grandpap always said, 'Put your heart into it and you'll be rewarded!' That's all I'm asking you kids to do."

I guess it wasn't impossible for Savanna, Mitchie and me to score nine goals in the second half. But that wouldn't do much good if our leaky goalkeeping failed to shut down the Dynamite's offensive assault.

"Who's goalkeeper?" I asked Grandpa Dan.

"Well, now, let me see..." Grandpa Dan looked around at the Bugs.

"I can't *ever* be the keeper!" Mitchie insisted. "My ma would kill me if I broke my new glasses!"

"Not me!" Fulton pleaded.

"I already did it!" Cary argued.

Several others shook their heads.

"Well now, someone's gotta play back there," Grandpa Dan reminded us.

When no one volunteered, I saw Savanna start to raise her hand. "I wi—"

"I'll do it!" She looked surprised when I loudly cut her off.

I felt bad about talking over her, but I didn't have a choice. Savanna was our only real striker. We couldn't afford to put her in goal!

So what if goalkeeper is my least favorite position on the field!

"That's the ticket, Rio!" Grandpa Dan clapped enthusiastically. "Rio will hold the fort and the rest of you Bugs fly at 'em like greased lightning!"

Grandpa Dan held out his right hand to start a team stack. But Savanna and I were the only ones who put our hands in.

If our soccer season was going to be saved, it was now or never! But I had no idea what to do.

Then I saw Savanna look straight at Grandpa Dan and give him a firm nod.

"Like Grandpa Dan's grandpap always said…" Savanna spoke in a steady voice, looking around the circle at each downcast face. "Put your heart into it…'"

She paused, waiting for the team to join in.

"You'll be rewarded." Mine was the only voice to join Savanna.

Savanna's eyes met mine. We both knew we were alone. Everyone else on the team had quit!

My eyes sank slowly to the ground… A large and deadly snake coiled around my stomach…

The Lightning Bugs were officially dead!

"Rome wasn't built in a day, kiddo!" Grandpa Dan reminded Savanna.

Savanna looked up… silent and unsure.

"Try it once more!" Grandpa Dan gave her one of his friendly little winks.

This time when Savanna spoke, her words were more like an order – a confident command.

"Put your heart into it–"

I hesitated for a second. Suddenly, a wave of voices filled my ears. "You'll be rewarded!"

It was *loud* this time – like everyone answered!

Grandpa Dan again held out his hand. Hands shot into the circle, quickly stacking on his.

"One, two, three!" he thundered.

"Lightning Bugs!" our voices echoed loudly.

When I took my place in front of the goal, I looked out at all the players lined up for the kickoff. The Dynamite kids were all wearing matching silver jerseys and shorts.

Since the Lightning Bugs were a brand new team, we hadn't gotten uniforms yet. We were all wearing plain white t-shirts.

It was pretty embarrassing – although nowhere near as embarrassing as losing by eight goals!

I stopped thinking about uniforms when Savanna stole a pass and quickly scored a goal on a breakaway to open the second half.

"Way to go, kiddo!" Grandpa Dan hollered from the sideline.

"Let's do it again, Lightning Bugs!" Mitchie pumped his fist in the air.

"Hubba-hubba!" I sang out as I did a ridiculous dance in the penalty box.

That was the last chance I had to celebrate the rest of the game. I was too busy diving, jumping, spinning, and blocking. I was determined to keep every Dynamite shot out of our goal!

And I almost succeeded.

Decatur bombarded our goal with 25 or 30 shots that I deflected with pretty much every body part – hands, feet, kneecap, elbow, armpit, nose, Adam's apple.

Meanwhile, Savanna put on a one-girl show, burning the Dynamite defenders with her incredible speed. She scored seven times in the second half – and Mitchie added another – to tie the score 10-10!

I readied myself as the Dynamite frontline bore down on our goal once more.

Their forward faked past Aurora and delivered a perfect cross to the striker. It was too far out in front for me to intercept, and Fulton was totally out of position.

The striker swung his leg and launched a missile toward the upper right corner of the goal.

Instinctively, I flipped feet-first into the air. The toe of my right foot barely grazed the speeding shot – but enough to deflect the ball away from the goal!

Unfortunately, it bounced right back to the striker. As I crash-landed against the right goalpost, he easily tapped the ball into the wide-open left side.

That was the only goal I surrendered, but it

was one too many!

With less than a minute to play, Grandpa Dan frantically waved at me to leave the goal box and join the final Lightning Bug attack.

I took off at full speed and, just as I reached midfield, took a push pass from Alton. I spotted Savanna streaking down the right sideline. There were too many Dynamite defenders in the way, so I lofted a chip over their heads.

Savanna gathered the ball in, spun, and blasted a power shot from twenty yards out.

It was a laser that froze the Dynamite keeper. All he could do was look up as the soccer ball zoomed over his head.

Every player on both teams stopped and watched as the ball hit the crossbar. It shot straight down and smacked the keeper dead-on in the face!

Blood exploded from his nose as the ball bounced out in front of the goal!

Everyone immediately flew into action, swarming toward the loose ball. But I had a clear path to it!

I raced forward and slid like a bullet train between two defenders. My right leg was fully extended, reaching out for the precious gem.

As I skidded across the grass, my foot made contact with the ball. I flicked it with my toe toward the goal! The final whistle blew almost at the same time!

I watched from the ground as my low-flying shot banged off the bloody keeper's shin and angled right into the net!

The referee waved his arms back and forth. "No goal! Game's over!"

The Dynamite players exploded – whooping and celebrating all around us.

All I could do was drive my fist into the turf in anger. We'd come so close! Even though I'd kicked the ball just before the final whistle, my shot had hit the keeper's leg a split-second after the ref had ended the game.

We lost 11-10!

I got to my feet and trudged toward our sideline. Out of the corner of my eye, I saw a blur racing in the opposite direction.

Savanna passed the goal line and kept running, toward the far end of the park.

I wanted to make sure she was okay, so I started after her.

When I caught up with her, Savanna was lying face down in the grass. Her shoulders heaved up and down, and I could hear her whimpering.

I stood there for a few seconds, not really knowing what to say or do.

"The Bugs played a great game," I finally offered.

Savanna didn't answer. I noticed the electronic devices weren't hooked behind her ears.

"Savanna?"

When she still didn't respond, I leaned down and lightly touched her shoulder.

Savanna immediately jerked up. When she saw it was me, she jumped to her feet. In each hand was one of her electronic ear things.

She saw me staring at them. "I didn't want to listen to them celebrating," she explained. She quickly hooked the devices behind each ear.

"I don't blame you," I said. I wanted to ask her about those hearing devices, but I didn't. I could tell from her red eyes that she'd been crying.

"Is everyone mad at me for missing that last shot?" Her face sank like some judge had just said she was guilty of armed robbery.

"Are you kidding?! You were the only reason we had a chance to win! That last shot would've gone in if the goalkeeper's big nose hadn't got in the way!"

Savanna looked at me and giggled. Before I knew what was happening, she flung her arms around me and gave me a giant hug. I don't usually hug girls, but there was nothing I could do about it.

Besides... all of a sudden, I felt way too good. I knew for sure our soccer season wasn't even close to going down the drain!

"Come on!" I grabbed Savanna's arm. "Grandpa Dan's taking us to get ice cream!"

The Lightning Bugs sat on a low brick wall outside the ice cream shop. Everyone had a cone with two big scoops.

Grandpa Dan was the last one to come out of the shop. He grinned from ear to ear as he marched toward us.

"To my never-say-die Lightning Bugs!" He raised his fudge ripple and banana coconut double-decker. "I take my hat off to you!"

"You're not wearing a hat, Grandpa Dan!" Mitchie laughed.

"Well, if I was, I'd take it off!" Grandpa Dan grinned merrily.

"Hubba-hubba!" Dawson shouted.

"Hubba-hubba!" everyone cheered.

Savanna sat on the wall next to me.

"You have a cool grandfather," she said and took a lick of ice cream. "He lives with you?"

I nodded. "With my mom and me."

"I wish my grandparents lived with us. But there's no way they'll ever leave Chicago." She paused to lick her cone, "They're on my dad's side. My mom's folks passed on before I was even born."

I nodded and licked my cone. I figured I should tell her, even though I knew it'd probably sound confusing.

"Grandpa Dan's not actually my grandpa."

"Oh?..." Savanna looked more curious than confused.

"I'm not even related to him. But he's like one of our family. For as long as I can remember, I've called him Grandpa Dan."

Savanna thought about it for a moment, then took another lick. "That's cool."

"Yeah..." I took another lick. "Can I ask you something?"

"Go for it," she immediately replied.

"Those, uh..." I didn't want to embarrass her, so I nodded toward her head.

Savanna spun around so I could get a good look at the back of her head. "You mean these?"

She took off one of the devices and held it out so I could examine it.

"It's a hearing aid, right?"

She shook her head. "Hearing aids are for people who can't hear very well. I can't hear at all."

"What's this part?" I pointed to the plastic hook piece that clipped behind her ear

"The processor. It has two tiny microphones that capture sounds."

"Would it work if I wore it?" I put it up to my ear.

Savanna giggled. "No, because you don't have an implant."

"A what?"

"See back here?" She pointed to her head just behind her ear. "I have a device implanted under my skin."

"For real?!"

She nodded and grinned. "It sends sound signals to my brain. This cable connects the processor to my implant."

"Wow! So… what happens when you take them off?"

Savanna took the processor off her other ear and laughed. "I'm deaf!"

"That's amazing!"

Savanna reattached one of the processors behind her ear. "What did you say?"

"Those things are amazing! You can just tune out the world whenever you want!"

"Yep! When my brother annoys me, I mute him!"

We both laughed and licked our ice cream cones.

Even though we lost a heartbreaker to Decatur, I was glad about two things – having a cool grandpa and a new friend!

-11-
Back Heel Pass

When we got home after the game, first thing I did was kick off my shoes and collapse on the couch. I heard Grandpa Dan coming toward the family room and figured he had the same idea.

But he was spinning a soccer ball on the tip of his finger. "How about I show you a new soccer trick?"

Even though I was exhausted, there was no way I could pass up an offer like that!

"It's called a back heel pass," Grandpa Dan explained. "It's one of the most difficult passes to master. But, oh, it's a thing of beauty when you pull it off!"

I watched as Grandpa Dan set the ball down about twenty yards from the goal. We were back at Lincoln Park and had the whole soccer field to ourselves – not counting the man-eating mosquitoes that were buzzing in large battalions this late in the day and so close to the river.

Grandpa Dan backed up, then started forward, dribbling the ball ahead of him. He picked up speed as he approached the goal. His right leg swung forward like he was going to attempt a shot.

Instead of blasting the ball into the net, Grandpa Dan's right leg stepped over the ball, landing out in front. At the same time, his left foot swung sideways under his body.

His left heel struck the side of the ball, sending it straight over to me.

Wow! The back heel pass *was* a thing of beauty! It was sure to make a fool of any defender or goalkeeper. I couldn't wait to try it!

Grandpa Dan moved over to the right as I dribbled the ball toward the goal. All I had to do was jump over the ball with my right foot, then pass the ball with my left heel. Grandpa Dan had made it look easy.

I swung my right leg like I was going to attempt a straight shot, then stepped over the ball. But instead of landing out in front of the ball like he did, my right foot landed on top of it. My ankle rolled and I sprawled awkwardly onto the ground.

"I know a guy who busted his ankle clear in two doing that!" Grandpa Dan chuckled as he helped me back to my feet. "Me!"

"For real?"

"Sure as Monday follows Sunday."

"What did I do wrong?"

"Pretty much everything. Next time, slow down the roll of the ball or try stepping a little farther out. Better yet, do both!"

My ankle hurt, but not enough to make me stop. This time I made sure my right foot cleared the ball. Unfortunately, when I swung my left foot under me, I kicked nothing but air!

"It's all about timing, son. Take another crack at it."

I took another crack, all right. For the next forty-five minutes, that's all I did. I didn't stop until I made ten back heel passes in a row with each foot.

"You've got it down!" Grandpa Dan finally proclaimed. "No two ways about it!"

"I can't wait to try it out in a game!"

"You may be waiting a while for that one."

"Huh? Why? You just said I got it down – no two ways about it!"

"I know I did. But a goalkeeper making a back heel pass is about as likely as a frog eating fried chicken with a knife and fork! Now, where'd I park that taxi?"

I had forgotten all about volunteering to play keeper!

"I only meant to be keeper for the first game. Not all season!" I protested.

"Well, in that case, maybe your pal, uh…"

"You mean Mitchie? Mitchie's mom won't let him play goalkeeper!"

"I guess we can put that little girl back in there again. The one with the, uh, head thing…" Grandpa Dan pointed at his forehead.

As we walked off the field, I remembered how badly outmatched Aurora and the two boys had been in goal against Decatur.

"It'd be another massacre," I muttered. "No matter who—"

"Doggone it!" Grandpa Dan interrupted as he rummaged through his pockets. "I *know* I put my keys in this pocket right here."

I tried to think of who else on the team might be able to play keeper. Alton? Sterling? Dawson? Nope. No way. And don't even *think* about it!

"Here they are! How'd they get in there?" Grandpa Dan pulled the keys from one of his vest pockets.

That meant I had to find someone who wasn't on the team. But, who? All the decent soccer players were already on teams.

Grandpa Dan seemed surprised when we walked up to the New Abe taxi. "Who parked it over here? Somebody must've moved it!"

As I climbed in the front seat, a light bulb suddenly went on in my brain. The Lightning Bugs' new keeper had to be someone who doesn't play soccer!

-12-
Long Shot

I ran into Quincy before school on Monday. He was sitting hunched over a calculator in the middle of the crowded upper-grade corridor as I headed for the boys bathroom.

"Q! We need to talk."

Quincy looked up excitedly. "The Sun travels 45,000 miles an hour, right?"

"Uh, last I checked."

"If we could go that fast, it would only take eight seconds to get from here to St. Louis!"

"Whoa, that's moving! How long would it take to get to the boys bathroom? Because that's where I'm headed."

"Hmmm… let me see…" Quincy actually started trying to figure it out on his calculator.

"That's okay, Q. We're here."

While Q worked the calculator buttons, I headed into the bathroom. Unfortunately, I bumped smack into the world's greatest soccer player.

"Get outta my way, loser!" Troy Niles ordered.

"Uh, hey, Troy," I mumbled.

I stepped way over to one side, giving Troy

enough room to drive a school bus out of the bathroom. But he moved over right with me. I guess he wanted to have a friendly little chat.

"How bad did you Mosquitoes lose on Saturday?"

"It's the Lightning Bugs."

"That's even worse! A slow-flying insect with a stupid lamp on its butt!"

"It's on the abdomen. Not that it matters."

Troy scowled and bumped his broad chest into my face, forcing me back into the hallway.

"Do you know how many goals I scored Saturday?"

Man, if only I could take off my sound processors like Savanna and mute this hyena!

"Um… zero?"

"Five! We won eight zip!"

"A real squeaker, huh?" I said with a straight face.

Teachers always say when kids like Troy act super tough it's because they're feeling some kind of pain inside. I don't know if that's true or not. All I know is that I always try to defend myself by turning everything he says into a joke.

"Do you have any clue how bad the Matrix are gonna destroy you pathetic little Lightning Bugs?"

"Lemme guess… one zip?"

"You're an idiot!" Troy paused for a moment. A cruel smile formed on his thin lips.

I started to squirm as I waited for his final attack. I knew exactly what the next word to come out of his mouth would be.

"Fido!" Troy spat out. Then he barked over and over. He barked loudly, so that the other kids in the hallway heard him and turned to stare at me.

I felt a sharp pain in my chest as Troy's mocking voice cut into me – just like Charlie Planck's sharp knife plunged into Abe Lincoln's dog. I looked down at my hands and quickly shoved them down deep into the pockets of my jeans before anyone could see Fido's blood.

Quincy looked up excitedly from his calculator. "Zero point zero-zero-zero-zero-one millisecond!"

"You're both idiots!" Troy snarled. He pushed us aside and stalked off.

"That's great, Q," I smiled weakly, still reeling from Troy's knife attack.

"Let's measure something else before the bell rings!" Quincy cleared the calculator and looked around for an idea.

"Actually, Q…" I reached out and took the calculator from Quincy's hand. "I have something more important to talk to you about."

"Like what? Robotics?!"

"More important than that." I led him toward the gym.

"Coding?"

I shook my head. "Still more important."

"Time travel?!"

"More important even than that."

"Nothing's more important than time travel," he pointed out.

I steered Quincy through the double doors into the gym. No one was around, just some frisbees and balls scattered on the floor.

"You know how you don't like to play sports?"

"What if I told you there's a sport where one player per team spends *all* his time figuring out math and time travel and stuff like that?"

Quincy's eyes lit up. "That would be so incredible!"

"Well, guess what? There *is* a sport like that!"

"You mean Math Olympics?"

"No, a real sport."

"Seriously?"

"Swear on day-old spit!" I held up my right hand like people do in court.

Quincy looked at me intently. "Swear on day-old baby slobber?"

"Baby slobber with banana chunks in it!" I

vowed. "I'd sure hate to see you lose out on this once-in-a-lifetime opportunity, Q!"

"Me, too!" Quincy agreed. "How come you get to do physics when you're supposed to be playing sports?"

"Well, because, uh… because you have to determine angles… and speed… and gravity! And it's all done at warp speed!"

Quincy's eyes widened. "Then I'll do it!" He couldn't believe his good fortune.

I gave Quincy a friendly slap on the back. "You'll be called the goalkeeper. Keeper, for short."

"Keeper…" Quincy had a dreamy look in his eyes. "What sport is it? Quidditch?""

"Better than quidditch." I used a toe kick to loft a soccer ball high up into the air. "It's the most popular sport in the world!"

Quincy glanced up and shot his hands over his head at the last second to deflect the ball away.

"Great save!" I gave Quincy a high five. Then I retrieved the ball and handed it to him. "Quincy the Keeper!" I crowed.

Quincy studied the black-and-white sphere as he spun it in his hands. "Wow… Twelve pentagons and twenty hexagons!" He looked up excitedly. "When do I get to start?"

"Today! We have practice after school!"

-13-
Keep the Keeper

I knew it was a total long shot that Quincy would succeed as our new goalkeeper. But I had zero options – and sometimes long shots hit the jackpot.

Most of the Lightning Bugs were busy doing passing drills with Grandpa Dan. Savanna, Mitchie, and I lined up along the top of the penalty box and booted shot after shot at the goal.

What the three of us witnessed is impossible to explain. For fifteen straight minutes not a single one of our shots reached the net! Not even Savanna's monster blasts! It was unbelievable!

Maybe it was because he's long, lean, and surprisingly quick – and because he can hyper-focus on things that interest him. Whatever the reason, Quincy Morrison was definitely born to be a goalkeeper!

"Geez, Quincy, you're too good!" Mitchie exclaimed.

"Yeah! You're like a force field!" Savanna added.

"It's just simple physics," Quincy explained. "Sir Isaac Newton's three laws of motion."

I could tell Mitchie and Savanna had no idea

what Quincy was talking about. I didn't know either.

Grandpa Dan trotted over to see how our newest teammate was faring. "So, are we gonna keep this keeper or what?"

"See for yourself," I told him.

The three of us each blasted a shot at the goal – and Quincy blocked them all!

"What rock have you been hiding under, son?" Grandpa Dan smiled broadly.

"Yeah!" Mitchie shouted. "We would'a beat Decatur if you'd been in goal!"

"And Rio said he's never played soccer before!" marveled Savanna.

"What's your secret, son?"

Quincy shrugged. "I just calculate velocity, lift and drag."

Grandpa Dan took off his red and white checkerboard cap and scratched his head.

"He's serious, Grandpa Dan!" I grinned.

Grandpa Dan put his hat back on and nodded at the goal. "Let me boot one at ya, son." He turned to me and held out his hand. "Hand me that, uh… that thing."

"The ball?" I was a little surprised that he forgot what it was called.

"Right." Grandpa Dan placed the ball on the grass, took two steps back, then launched a banana kick that screamed around Quincy's outstretched hands into the net.

"Hubba-hubba!" Savanna exclaimed.

"This old dog's got a little life in him yet!" Grandpa Dan chuckled.

"I forgot all about the Magnus effect," Quincy moaned.

"The what?" Mitchie asked.

"The Magnus effect is what makes a ball curve when you kick it off-center," Quincy explained.

"Right," Mitchie agreed, looking totally mystified.

The Lightning Bugs spent the rest of practice working on the triangle offense.

I'd never really thought about triangles much, except in school when we were studying math. But I could see how a soccer team would just be a random bunch of disconnected parts without a solid structure.

And Grandpa Dan had said the triangle is the strongest structure on earth!

Mr. Niles never mentioned triangles or any other geometric shapes at Matrix practices. He just told everyone to spread out and let Troy control the ball. I guess when you win every game there's not much reason to change your strategy.

The sun had sunk below the cornfields, and it was getting almost too dark to practice. Sterling, Dawson, and Aurora chased after some lightning bugs that were playing hide-and-seek a few feet above the grass.

Grandpa Dan rounded up all the kids into a circle. Dawson showed us a lightning bug that she cradled in her open hand. Its tiny yellow light shone brightly for a second and went out.

"Know what their light is for?" Grandpa Dan asked us.

"Attracting mates," Quincy responded.

I knew our new keeper would be all over that answer.

Grandpa Dan smiled as the little lamp flashed again. "The light also warns predators like birds and bats to stay away. These little guys have a chemical inside their bodies that has a terrible taste."

Quincy leaned closer toward Dawson's palm. "I wonder how bad?" He looked like he wanted to find out.

"Bad enough to trigger vomiting!" Grandpa Dan hooted as Quincy pulled back.

The bug crawled toward Dawson's thumb, then took off into the air. Its little light winked at us as it slowly flew away.

"I've never tried to count 'em all, but I

swear there aren't as many of those magical little creatures as when I was a boy," Grandpa Dan told us.

"What happened to them?" asked Dawson.

"Who knows?" Grandpa Dan shrugged. "Mother Nature is changing. Not always for the better."

"It's called climate change," said Quincy.

"Whatever it is, you Lightning Bugs are becoming a rare breed. So, you need to stay strong. 'Specially on Saturday when we play, uh…" Grandpa Dan turned to me. "Who're we playing, son?"

"Bloomington Fire."

"Right. The Fire… Now, here's the thing that you kids from New Abe need to remember about fire." Grandpa Dan motioned us closer, like he was about to tell us an important secret. "Fire burned down our town!"

"It did?" asked Cary. He looked around at the houses next to the park.

"I read about that!" Quincy said excitedly. "New Abe was built right on top of the ashes of the old town of Abe, Illinois!"

Grandpa Dan nodded. "1887 – a lightning strike. The bolt hit the old firehouse, of all places!"

"For real?" Dawson squealed.

"Real as Sunday follows Monday."

Sunday follows Monday? The other kids were too busy thinking about the big fire to notice Grandpa Dan's flub.

"Once the firehouse burned to the ground," Grandpa Dan continued, "everything else in town went with it!"

"Wow!" several voices murmured.

Grandpa Dan held out his right hand and everyone made a hand stack.

"If you kids play as hard as you did in that first game... and with this hot-shot professional keeper defending our goal... the Bloomington Fire's gonna get their goose cooked on Saturday!"

I could see in my teammates' eyes that they were starting to believe it.

"One, two, three!" Grandpa Dan shouted.

"Hubba-hubba!" we all yelled, swinging our hands up to the sky.

-14-
Direct Hit

Bloomington isn't as big a town as Springfield, but it's still big compared to New Abe. They have a 13-story office building that you can see way before you even get to town. They also have three multiplex movie theaters. And that's just the ones I know of. I wouldn't be surprised if there are two or three more.

Best of all, Bloomington has a soccer complex with twelve playing fields! Wherever you look, a thousand kids or more are playing soccer.

Savanna laughed when I talked about being impressed by the size of everything in Bloomington.

"You're kidding, right?"

"Well, not big like Chicago," I tried to explain. "Big like, uh… Peoria."

That made her laugh even more. You must have to be from a big city like Chicago to find Peoria that hilarious.

Savanna, Mitchie, and I stood in a triangle, passing a ball back and forth. The other Bugs were doing the same. Except Quincy. He was busy with his calculator.

The Fire warmed up at the other end of the

field. They wore black uniforms with cool orange flames on the front.

The Lightning Bugs were all still wearing plain white t-shirts. I'd asked Grandpa Dan about getting some team jerseys, but he didn't seem interested in how we looked.

I wasn't surprised. Grandpa Dan didn't care about things like clothes. He wore that same old checkerboard hat and vest pretty much every day.

"Can't judge a book by its cover," he liked to say. I knew deep down he was right. But I still wished we had something better to wear than crummy white t-shirts.

The referee blew her whistle and signaled for the two teams to get ready for the opening kickoff.

The Fire's coach huddled with his players. I looked around the sideline, but didn't immediately see Grandpa Dan.

The Fire broke the huddle and raced to their positions on the field. All the Lightning Bugs just stood around the sideline looking at each other.

The ref waved at us. "Get moving, New Abe!"

I looked all around, but Grandpa Dan still was nowhere to be seen! I could feel a knot forming in my stomach. Grandpa Dan might be a big joker, but he wouldn't just leave right when the match was starting!

Unless a customer called and said they needed a taxi right now!

I wasn't even sure it was legal for us to play without a coach there. But maybe no one would notice since there were plenty of parents standing along the sideline.

"Huddle up!" I called out.

All the Bugs trotted over and formed a lopsided circle around me.

"Where's Grandpa Dan?" asked Dawson.

The other kids stood there, waiting for me to answer. The knot in my stomach was getting tighter.

"Uh…"

The ref blasted her whistle to get us moving.

"Here's the starting lineup," I said quickly. "Savanna and Mitchie are the forwards. Alton and Aurora wingers. I'm center mid. Sterling and Cary on defense. Q in goal."

"I've never played winger before," Aurora said in a nervous voice.

"No worries, you'll be fine," I told her. "Just stay over on my right. When the ball comes to you, kick it to me or Savanna."

Grandpa Dan and I had spent a lot of time discussing how to best use Aurora. We wanted her to play her share, but without totally messing things up.

We'd decided to put her on the wing. That way I could cover for her if she got into trouble.

Savanna had a quizzical look on her face. "Where *is* Grandpa Dan?"

Before I could think of what to say, we heard a familiar voice calling out.

"Over here, Bugs!"

Everyone turned and saw… Grandpa Dan walking from his taxi in the parking lot. He was carrying a large cardboard box.

All the Bugs took off running toward him. As we pulled up around him, Grandpa Dan reached into the box and started handing out new soccer jerseys!

"Put 'em on over your t-shirts!"

The jerseys were red and white checkerboard, just like the taxi! They looked great!

The new uniforms seemed to fill all the Lightning Bugs with a burst of energy. We raced back onto the field to get the party started!

As soon as the match started, the Fire were on the attack. They had beaten Macomb in their first match, and it was obvious they were an experienced unit.

They flooded our half with attackers. It seemed impossible for us to even clear the ball past mid-field.

Somehow, we managed to stop every scoring opportunity. I didn't know if it was the new uniforms… or having Quincy in goal… or what. But long gone were the defensive woes that doomed us last week against Decatur. The game's first ten minutes were scoreless.

That ended when I intercepted a pass from a winger and dribbled the ball into Fire territory. On my right was Savanna. Mitchie raced in from the left.

One of the defenders came at me, so I quickly side passed to Mitchie. As expected, the second defender immediately went for Mitchie.

"Mitchie!" I called as I looped behind him. My defender followed me, just as I'd hoped.

Mitchie faked a pass back to me, then delivered a perfect strike to Savanna, who was unguarded on the right.

Before the goalkeeper could react, Savanna one-timed Mitchie's pass into the right corner of the goal!

Savanna's goal opened the floodgates. Two minutes later, Mitchie's indirect free kick bounced off Dawson's shin. I gathered it in, dribbled around a defender, and drilled the ball into the back of the net.

On the next kickoff, Alton stole the ball

from a Fire winger and crossed it to Savanna. She trapped the pass with the bottom of her shoe, dribbled between two defenders, and froze the keeper by faking a shot to the right. When he dove for the fake, Savanna easily punched the ball into the wide-open left side of the goal.

Meanwhile, Quincy was a total brick wall in our goal. Every shot the Fire took he caught or deflected away, or he just booted the ball back to midfield.

Our two defenders, Sterling and Cary, had been nonexistent in our first game. But today, they helped Q out by blocking several shots. Sterling even intercepted two crosses.

Savanna finished off the half by heading my corner kick into the net. One of her sound processors flew off when her head struck the ball, but Alton caught it.

Grandpa Dan did a little jig as he greeted us on the sideline.

"Four zip! Mmm-mmm..." He rubbed his stomach hungrily. "I just love the smell of cooked goose!"

It was a warm and super humid day, so we all gulped water and sprawled out on the grass to rest.

I looked up and noticed some afternoon thunderclouds forming overhead. That concerned me.

Not that we might get rained on. I didn't care about that. But if the match was called off, we wouldn't get the win!

"Hey, Grandpa Dan, does the game count if it gets cancelled because of weather?" Mitchie was thinking the same thing.

Grandpa Dan glanced up at the sky and frowned. "I don't know, son. Every league has its own rules."

He went over to talk to the referee. I felt a raindrop hit my shoulder.

When Grandpa Dan came back, he waved at us to hurry and get up.

"As long as we start the second half, the game counts!"

I looked up again at the sky and saw a flash of lightning high above the clouds. It was so high up, there wasn't any thunder.

"Did you see that?!" Quincy exclaimed. "A sprite halo! Those are totally rare!"

The wind picked up as the Bugs dashed onto the field. Raindrops fell more steadily. A storm was definitely moving in.

We stood at our positions for the kickoff. We were ready, the referee was ready, but it seemed like the Fire were taking an extra long time breaking their huddle on the sideline.

I saw their coach glance up at the sky, then continue taking to his players. It was obvious they were stalling. They were hoping to get the game cancelled before the second half began.

The ref blasted her whistle, but it was drowned out by the wind. If the Bloomington players heard it, they acted like they hadn't.

I looked up as lightning flashed lower in the deep purple sky. This time the rumble of distant thunder followed.

The ref trotted over to the Fire huddle and said something that finally got them moving. As the Fire players strolled slowly onto the field, lightning flashed again.

"C'mon! Hurry up!" I said between clenched teeth. The second half would start – and the game would count – as soon as one of the Fire kicked the ball!

Their striker walked up to the center circle. He looked down at the ball and frowned like there was something wrong with it. He picked the ball up, spun it around in his hands, then set it back down right where it had been.

I glanced up again. The thunderclouds overhead looked darker and angrier by the second!

The Fire striker was sure taking his sweet time! He looked over at his coach, then turned and said something to a teammate. They both looked up at the sky and held out their hands to catch raindrops.

The referee blew her whistle again. She motioned at the striker to kick the ball.

He nodded and swung his left leg, but froze just before his foot touched the ball.

The Lightning Bugs all started yelling at the Fire striker and at the ref.

"Kick it!... He's cheating!... They're just trying not to lose!"

The ref motioned at him again to kick the ball.

The striker nodded and walked over to the other side of the ball, then walked back to where he'd started.

"Kick it!" the Bugs all screamed in frustration.

When the striker started walking around the ball again, the referee suddenly ran forward blowing her whistle. She ordered the striker out of the center circle, then pointed at another Fire forward to do the kickoff.

The other kid shrugged and stepped into the center circle. I figured he would stall just like the striker. Without hesitating, he passed the ball to a teammate.

A second later, a deafening explosion nearly knocked me off my feet!

I spun around and saw a bolt of lightning strike our goal post! Quincy was standing motionless directly in front of the goal. His hair was sticking straight up! A jagged current of electricity danced inches above his head!

The lightning flash was so intense, I had to squeeze my eyelids shut! The last thing I saw was Quincy crumpling to the ground!

The sky suddenly opened up and rain began pounding us with fury! Everyone on all twelve soccer fields started yelling and screaming and running for shelter!

I was totally drenched when I reached our goal. "Q! You okay?!"

Quincy looked up at me, his eyes were bugged out wide. "That was a direct hit! Right next to me!"

"I know!"

"I could feel it vibrate up from my feet and out the top of my head!"

More thunder rumbled across the purple black sky.

I grabbed Quincy by the arm and pulled him to his feet. "Let's get out of here before it strikes again!"

Quincy didn't budge. He was staring in awe at the charred goal post. "Lightning's three times hotter than the surface of the Sun!"

"Great, Q, great! Now, come on!" I tugged at his arm, desperately wanting to get to the taxi.

Grandpa Dan suddenly appeared. "Thank heavens you're alive!"

"I wonder if I'll have magical powers now!" Quincy said.

"You already have magical powers, son! You're the best darn goalkeeper I've ever laid eyes on!"

We turned and raced through the puddles on the now-empty field. Another bolt of lightning exploded directly over our heads.

Quincy stopped and looked up. "Hey! I just thought of something. The Lightning Bugs actually won twice!"

"Huh?" I asked.

He grinned. "We beat the Fire... *and* we beat the lightning!"

-15-
Drifting Away

Grandpa Dan blasted the taxi horn and waved at folks as we drove back into New Abe after the match.

"The Lightning Bugs won!" he yelled out the window.

I'm not sure people knew what that meant, but they smiled and waved back anyway.

I didn't feel bad about winning the way we did. We beat Bloomington fair and square, even if the match was called early. If we'd played the whole second half, we probably would've beaten them by eight or nine goals!

We drove right past the ice cream shop. When I saw Grandpa Dan wasn't going to stop, I knew I had to act fast.

"Let's bring Mom an ice cream cone! She's probably hot after working all day."

"Great idea, son!"

Grandpa Dan licked his double-decker as we drove home. I held my cone in one hand and Mom's in the other.

For some reason, we stopped at the corner a block from the house. Grandpa Dan looked left and right, but didn't drive, even though no traffic was in sight. He just frowned and peered down both streets.

Mom's ice cream was beginning to drip onto my fingers. "Is something wrong with the taxi, Grandpa Dan?"

He jerked like I'd startled him. "No, son, no! I'm just trying to figure out which way to go."

"The house is right over there!" I started to laugh, until I realized that maybe he wasn't joking.

"Right!" Grandpa Dan zoomed off. "Glad I've got my co-pilot with me!" He laughed and slapped my knee.

I smiled back at him, but inside I was feeling uneasy. "Is everything okay, Grandpa Dan?"

"Sure, son! I'm just getting a little forgetful, is all. That's what happens when you get older." Grandpa Dan slowed down, searching the row of houses. He suddenly grinned as ours came into view.

"There she is! Home sweet home!"

Pike and I were lying on my bed. I was reading a soccer book about some kids in Iowa and he was sleeping in a pool of drool. Pike's not what you'd call a reading fanatic, but he sure can produce saliva!

Mom tapped on the door and poked her head

into the room.

"Thanks again for the ice cream."

"Sure, Mom. Sorry it was more like soup."

"It was delicious – and fun drinking it with a straw!"

She came over to sit on the edge of the bed. I knew that meant she wanted to talk about something, so I put the book down.

"Rio, have you noticed anything different about Grandpa Dan?"

One good thing about talking to Mom is that she doesn't ever waste your time. She gets right to the point. I guess she learned that working in an emergency room.

"I don't know."

"Like him forgetting things?"

"A little," I shrugged. "I guess he's just getting old, huh?"

"I'm afraid it's more than just getting old."

My whole body tensed up when she said that. I could tell by the worried look on her face that she was about to tell me something bad. Maybe *real* bad.

Mom put her hand on mine. "Grandpa Dan has a disease, *mijo*."

She squeezed my hand when she said it, but my chest is what felt tight. Something was pressing down on it hard – so hard I could barely breathe.

"What… disease?" I finally asked, unsure I could even bear to hear the answer.

"It's called Alzheimer's. It attacks the brain, making it harder to remember things and to think clearly."

I slumped forward. I'd heard about that disease from Chestnut Berwick. Her grandma has it. Chestnut said her grandma doesn't even know who she is anymore!

Mom put her arm around my shoulder. "It's going to get more difficult for him, *mijo*."

"How bad?" I barely squeaked. Tears were starting to burn my eyes.

"We don't know. And we don't know how quickly it will all happen."

That explains why Grandpa Dan hasn't called me Rio for I don't know how long! From now on, I'm just *son*, like every other kid in town!

It's embarrassing to admit this, but as I sat there all wet-eyed and miserable, the person I felt the most sorry for was… *myself*.

It felt like Grandpa Dan was leaving me behind… abandoning me… like he didn't care about me anymore!

I knew it was wrong to be angry at Grandpa Dan for having a disease that he never asked for. But I couldn't help feeling that way! I couldn't lose another dad!

"Does Grandpa Dan know he's got it?" I finally whispered.

Mom shook her head, handing me a tissue. "He's been told, but he doesn't remember."

"He couldn't remember the way home today!"

"I was afraid that would happen. He's not going to be able to drive that taxi much longer."

"But, that'll kill him, Mom!"

"I know, *mijo*. But he'll get to the point where he won't remember the taxi either."

I couldn't believe this was happening! It was like a nightmare that you know is *never* going to end! Tears streamed down my cheeks. But they weren't for me. All I cared about was Grandpa Dan!

"What's gonna happen to him?!"

Mom put both arms around me and held me tightly.

"Isn't there anything we can do?" I begged her.

"The most important thing for us is to be Grandpa Dan's anchor – when he starts to drift farther away."

Rivers of tears were running down Mom's cheeks too. I put my arms around her and... we held each other as we cried.

-16-
Hat Trick

For the next few weeks, Grandpa Dan didn't seem much different. At least, not that I could tell. Mostly he just couldn't remember the names of things – people's names and regular, ordinary items, like the stove and car keys.

I started hoping that the disease had gotten as bad as it was going to get. I was already planning on making a bunch of labels for everything. Then Grandpa Dan could just read the label if he forgot what it was called!

No one on the team seemed to notice anything different about him. If they did, they didn't make a big deal about it.

Soccer practices were as fun as always. If Grandpa Dan forgot target practice or some other wacky drill he'd taught us, the team would just automatically do it.

And the other kids were getting real good at understanding Grandpa Dan's peculiar sayings. When he hollered, "Keep your eyes peeled!" or "Get on the same page!" the Bugs knew he wanted them to focus and play as a single unit.

To the surprise of everyone in the Central

Illinois League, the Lightning Bugs went on a winning streak! I think even Grandpa Dan was amazed – even though he acted like he expected it all along.

After our lightning-strike victory in Bloomington, the Bugs made it two in a row by shutting out the Peoria Pride three zip.

Savanna scored a pair of goals in the first half – both on big-bending banana kicks. Grandpa Dan had shown her how to bend her shots, and it didn't take Savanna long at all to master it.

In the game's final minute, I closed down on the Peoria center mid and stole the ball with a quick swipe of my foot. As the center mid stepped out to try to regain possession, I drilled a killer pass right through his legs that Savanna one-touched into the net.

Once again, Quincy was a total freak in the goal. His arms and legs shot out so fast in every direction, it was unreal!

"Force equals mass times acceleration!" he'd shout out to no one in particular as he blocked one shot after another.

Our fourth game of the season was nearly canceled by an insect invasion!

It had been scorching hot in Illinois for two straight weeks – 100 degrees or more everyday!

Even the nights were sweltering and sticky. Not a single drop of rain had fallen in Sangamon County or anywhere else around here since the nearly fatal lightning storm in Bloomington.

Dry blades of grass crunched as we walked onto the soccer field in Normal. The entire field was brown and brittle.

The Cardinals were warming up at the far goal, but I wasn't paying any attention to them. I couldn't take my eyes off the field!

That's because, for a split-second, it looked like the field was moving! Maybe it was just sun glare, but the soccer field kind of looked like a mega-flat furry brown turf monster!

That's when I realized it *was* moving! All that crunching under my feet wasn't just dry grass.

"Grasshoppers!" Mitchie yelled.

We all stopped and stared down at the ground in disbelief... Millions of grasshoppers! Same color as the dried grass!

Wait! I wasn't sure there even *was* any grass! The field might be *all* grasshoppers!

Around here, we always see plenty of grasshoppers every summer. But nothing insane like this!

The Lightning Bugs forgot all about warming up for the match. Everyone was too busy scooping up grasshoppers.

"Oh, they're so cute!" Aurora gushed.

"I love you, Mr. Grasshopper!" Dawson cooed.

"Mr. Locust," Quincy corrected her.

"Huh?" Dawson asked.

"Grasshoppers that swarm are called locusts." He picked one up in his hand and carefully studied it. "I wonder what locusts taste like?"

A grasshopper jumped up onto my knee and spit some disgusting brown juice that trickled down my leg.

"Kind of salty and fishy," Quincy said as he pulled an antenna from between his front teeth.

Grandpa Dan walked up beside me.

"Is it true grasshoppers bring bad luck?" I asked him.

"Farmers say that, not that I blame them. But I never found it to be the case."

Grandpa Dan stooped down and held out his hand. As I watched, several grasshoppers jumped up onto it. He grinned like a little kid.

The only one who didn't seem to be enjoying the swarm of locusts was Savanna. Eyes wide and unblinking, she stood on her tiptoes like she was trying not to come in contact with the insects.

"I think one flew up my nose!" she shrieked

in horror.

"Plug your other nostril and blow it out!" I told her, trying not to smile.

She did – and the sticky grasshopper shot out of her nose like a dive-bombing vampire bat.

"Ooh–! How disgusting!" Savanna looked like she was going to be sick.

I've blown plenty of bugs out of my nose, but I guess they don't have insect invasions in a paved-over city like Chicago.

A loud roaring sound suddenly grabbed our attention. Across the field, some park workers were standing next to a gigantic fan on wheels.

We all watched in amazement as the powerful fan lifted thousands of grasshoppers off the field and blew them over the sideline! Then the workers repositioned the fan and started clearing off the rest of the field. Another low brown cloud of insects floated away!

"We do this before every game!" one of the guys explained to Grandpa Dan.

Once the match finally started, the Cardinals probably wished that guy had turned the giant fan on the Lightning Bugs. Savanna and Mitchie scored five first half goals, and we cruised to a 6-0 victory!

Most of the players took grasshoppers home. Quincy wanted to study their anatomy. Dawson and Sterling said they were rescuing them from the giant fan. Mitchie wanted one as a pet and even gave it a name – Leo Messi. Two grasshoppers snuggled in Aurora's headband.

Savanna and I were the only ones who didn't take any. She, for obvious reasons. Me, because I didn't want to get spit on again. Besides, I'd hate to see our soccer field at Lincoln Park turn into a mega-flat furry brown turf monster!

Quincy the Great Wall of China finally surrendered his first goal of the season against the Macomb Zips. The Zips had only won one game all season because their defense was like Swiss cheese. Their striker, however, was almost as talented as Troy Niles.

Quincy blocked about fifteen rocket blasts before the Macomb striker drilled one right between Q's legs. By the time Quincy's knees banged together, the ball was in the back of the net.

Quincy couldn't believe it. He just stood there bent over at the waist, staring through his legs at the ball nestled in the goal net.

"Take a good look, Q!" I trotted up alongside him. "Probably be the last one ever gets by you!"

Some keepers let it get under their skin

when they give up a goal, but not Quincy. He just increased his hyper-focus, kept chanting physics equations, and saved the next twenty shots!

The Lightning Bugs trounced the Zips 7-1!

The Central Illinois Soccer League website posted the standings after every week's games. I studied the list until I had it memorized.

Springfield Matrix	*5-0*
Danville Twisters	*4-1*
New Abe Lightning Bugs	*4-1*
Bloomington Fire	*3-3*
Peoria Pride	*3-3*
Normal Cardinals	*2-3*
Decatur Dynamite	*2-3*
Macomb Zips	*1-5*
Champaign Comets	*0-5*

Four wins in a row! We were tied with Danville for second place!

The cellar-dwelling Champaign Comets came to Lincoln Park for our sixth game. The Comets had won a single match all season. Last week, the Matrix totally crushed them 19-0! Troy Niles broke a league record with eleven goals!

My teammates were horsing around more

than usual during pre-game warm-ups. I knew the Comets probably wouldn't be much competition, but the Bugs seemed a little too relaxed – like the game had already been won just by showing up.

Grandpa Dan must've noticed it too, because he had some unusually stern words for us when we huddled on the sideline before the opening kickoff.

"I guarantee you, those kids over there are gonna come out swinging. A hungry team is a dangerous team! If you relax, they'll eat you alive!"

"Don't worry, Grandpa Dan," Mitchie grinned. "We like winning too much to go easy on them!"

"Actions speak louder than words, son. Now, everyone get your hands in here!"

All the kids piled their hands on top of Grandpa Dan's.

"One, two, three!"

"Hubba-hubba..." Even our cheer sounded lazy.

As we started out onto the field, Grandpa Dan stopped me.

"Hold on a sec, uh..., uh..."

"Rio," I reminded him.

Grandpa Dan said something about the kickoff, but I didn't really hear him.

That's because my heart was sinking. Grandpa Dan really didn't remember my name anymore!

I guess the Comets were sick and tired of losing. As soon as the game started, it was like we were running in slo-mo and they were on fast-forward. If it hadn't been for Quincy, the game would have been all but over by halftime.

The Comets bombarded our goal with so many shots, it was inevitable that a few of them would find the net. Three of them did. The last one, Quincy accidentally kicked in an own goal.

The Lightning Bugs trailed at the half three zip. It was the first time we were behind at halftime since the season opener.

Grandpa Dan didn't need to tell us what the problem was. We didn't give him a chance.

"We're sleepwalking out there!" Mitchie hollered.

"Nobody's hustling! Including me!" added Savanna.

"And we totally forgot about making triangles!" Sterling moaned.

"Three goals!... I really messed up Sir Isaac Newton's laws!" Quincy mourned.

"It's not your fault, Q!" I told him and everyone else. "We didn't help you at all! We didn't help anyone – except the Comets!"

When everyone had finished complaining, we waited for Grandpa Dan to rip into us. But when I looked over at him, he was grinning!

Oh, no… He must've already forgotten the score!

"Glad to see you kids are finally ready to play some soccer," he said calmly. "That's good because, I don't know about you, but I don't like the smell of my own goose cooking."

Every Lightning Bug nodded agreement, their faces filling with grim determination.

I was the only one smiling. I tried to hide it, but I was way too happy.

Grandpa Dan knew exactly what had happened in that first half!

From the moment of the second half kickoff, the Lightning Bugs were the ones playing on fast-forward.

Savanna stutter-stepped around three Comet midfielders, then chipped the ball over the head of the last defender and sped around him to maintain possession!

The Comets goalkeeper steadied herself as Savanna took aim at the near post. The soccer ball exploded off Savanna's right foot. Unfortunately, it flew straight into the keeper's raised hands!

But the ball was traveling so fast, it practically tore off the keeper's gloves! The ball and the goalkeeper landed in the back of the net, cutting the Comets lead to 3-1.

On the very next possession, one of the Comets midfielders dribbled around Alton and ran with the ball toward our goal. The attacking midfielder had a forward on either side.

I sped at an angle toward the kid with the ball. Our defenders, Sterling and Cary, spread out to cover the forwards.

I saw with alarm that Quincy was bent over in front of the goal tying his shoe!

"Q!" I yelled.

He looked up, but it was too late. The Comets midfielder swung his leg to shoot at the unguarded goal.

My only hope was to try a desperate, last-second slide tackle. I launched forward, skidding across the grass with my left foot stretched out. Just as the midfielder made contact with the ball, I pushed it away.

I slid back to my feet with the ball still balanced on my toe! I turned my head and saw Dawson dashing up the left flank. Before the Comets defense could react, I sent a weighted pass to start our counterattack.

Dawson gathered it in and quickly passed

the ball upfield to Alton. He blew past a midfielder and sped into Comets territory.

Mitchie moved to the center of the penalty area. Savanna raced in from the right to complete the triangle.

Alton delivered a perfect push pass to Mitchie, then took off toward the goal.

When the two Comet defenders converged on Mitchie, he sent the ball right back to Alton.

Alton took the pass and faked a shot. The keeper bit. Alton delivered the ball across the goal area to Savanna. All she had to do was stick out her foot and redirect the bouncing ball into the net! That narrowed the Comets lead to 3-2.

The Comets sensed that the tide had turned. On the next kickoff, their center mid panicked and passed the ball right to Dawson.

Dawson stuck out her foot and one-touched it to Fulton, who did the same, one-touching the ball to me! Just the way Grandpa Dan had taught us. It was a thing of beauty!

I took Fulton's pass in full stride and angled toward the left post.

The goalkeeper shifted over to block me. Out of the corner of my eye, I could see Savanna quickly closing in from the right.

I could've just hit the brakes and crossed the ball over to her. Instead, I decided to try something a little trickier. Actually a lot trickier – the back heel pass Grandpa Dan had taught me!

I didn't want to mess everything up by making the pass too soon. I needed the keeper to think I was going to take the shot, then at the last second send it over to Savanna for a wide open goal!

I dribbled closer, then swung my right leg back as if to shoot.

The keeper took the bait and dove to block my shot.

As my right foot swung above the rolling soccer ball, I swung my left foot under my body.

Even though I couldn't see behind me, I could feel my left foot miraculously make contact with the ball!

Savanna's eyes grew big as the ball rolled toward her. All the goalkeeper could do was turn and watch helplessly as Savanna kicked the ball into the net.

Just like that, the scored was tied! Savanna had scored three goals – a hat trick – in less than five minutes!

The rapid-fire Lightning Bugs offensive attack that tied the score seemed to take all the life out of the Comets. The energy they had shown in the first half completely drained out of them.

Savanna scored two more goals and I added

one when the Comets goalkeeper shanked a punt. I controlled the kick with my chest, then took on the sole defender by dribbling right at him. With a quick feint, I got him to turn left. I blew by his right and drilled the ball into the net before the keeper could get back in goal.

The final score was 6-3!

Everyone gathered around Grandpa Dan on the sideline. We jumped up and down and began a crazy victory dance.

"Hubba-hubba!" Our ten voices were anything but lazy.

-17-
Lost!

Only two weeks remained in the soccer season. The Lightning Bugs were still in the Central Illinois League top three!

Springfield Matrix	*6-0*
Danville Twisters	*5-1*
New Abe Lightning Bugs	*5-1*
Bloomington Fire	*3-3*
Peoria Pride	*3-3*
Normal Cardinals	*3-4*
Decatur Dynamite	*2-4*
Macomb Zips	*1-6*
Champaign Comets	*0-6*

Our final two games were against the league's two best teams – Danville Twisters and Springfield Matrix.

That was perfect! If we won those last two games, the Lightning Bugs would be the league champs!

Even though the Bugs and the Matrix would have identical 7-1 records, we'd be champs because we beat them in head-to-head competition! I know because Quincy and I already did the research.

Grandpa Dan was out driving the taxi, so I headed to the backyard with my soccer ball to see if Pike wanted to scrimmage.

Pike wasn't much good at passing or shooting, but he sure could play defense! When I'd try to dribble across the backyard, Pike would chase me, bump into me, and slobber all over the ball!

The way I figured it, if I could make it all the way across the yard against Pike and his tenacious D, any defender in the Central Illinois League would be a piece of cake!

Pike was raring to go, as usual. The first time I started dribbling, that crazy dog cut right in front of me. Our feet got tangled. I lost my balance and face-planted onto the grass!

Next time, I made it about halfway across the yard when Pike decided to sit on the ball! I tried kicking it out from under him, but that dog weighs at least fifty pounds!

On my third attempt, I faked left and Pike fell for it. I shot past him and dribbled the ball at full-speed. I could hear him barking hot on my heels!

As I neared the opposite end of the yard, Pike suddenly barreled right between my legs. I fell back and came down with my bottom on his back. I rode him like a champion bull rider for about five seconds!

Pike finally sped out from under me and I landed in a heap, laughing like crazy. Pike came over and started slobbering all over my face, which made me laugh even harder!

"Rio! Rio, come here! Quick!"

I could tell by the sound of Mom's voice that she meant business, so I got up right away and trotted to the back door.

Mom was on the phone. "No, no! Stay right where you are! Don't get out of the taxi! We're on our way!" She grabbed her keys without even looking at me. "Get in the car!"

I chased her through the living room. "What's going on, Mom?"

She charged out the front door, yelling over her shoulder, "Grandpa Dan's lost!"

We sped down the old two-lane river road toward Springfield. Mom drove faster than I'd ever seen her drive! She squeezed the steering wheel, eyes frantically searching left and right.

"I knew this would happen! I should have hidden his keys!"

"If Grandpa Dan's lost, how do you know where to go?!"

"I don't! He just said he's on a dirt road by the river! He was coming back from taking a customer to Springfield!"

The highway runs parallel to the Sangamon, but the river twists and turns so much that sometimes you can't even see it from the road. Plus, a forest of oak, hickory, and sycamore crowd the rich black soil between the highway and the river.

"Can't you try to call him again, Mom?"

"His battery's dead – or he's just not answering anymore!"

I gulped hard and searched out the window for the dirt road. The problem was, once you turned off the highway, every back road in Sangamon County was dirt or gravel.

To make matters worse, the sun was setting behind the cornfields that rippled like an endless green ocean to the west! Another hour of daylight this time of year – then it would get *real* dark out here!

Our tires squealed as Mom made a sudden turn off the highway. The car bumped almost out of control onto an unpaved one-lane road that was immediately swallowed by trees.

"Why'd you turn here?"

"Stop asking questions! *Madre mia!* I don't know what else to do!"

I shut my mouth, but didn't take offense at the way Mom snapped at me. She may be an ER nurse, but I could tell she was just as scared and stressed out as I was.

The dirt road narrowed and became more deeply rutted. Trees and bushes pressed against us so tightly, I didn't know if we'd be able to turn around and get out of here!

"Oh, we're just wasting time! He's not here!" Mom hit the brakes and at the same time jerked the gear shifter into reverse. We started backing up – fast!

"Mom!" I pointed through the trees. "There's something red!"

She slammed the brakes again.

"Where?! Did you see him?!"

"Over there! I think! I'm not sure!"

She sped forward again. Instead of slowing down as we approached a swampy stretch, Mom hit the gas! Muddy water sprayed out from both sides as the car sped through the muck!

I searched in every direction, but I didn't see anything red in the woods now.

"Where is it, Rio?!" Mom yelled.

"I don't know!"

The car bounced around a sharp bend. We came up a sudden rise – Mom screamed and stomped on the brakes. I grabbed the dash to keep from flying into the windshield.

"*Madre mia*!" she screamed, staring straight ahead.

The narrow road abruptly ended – the Sangamon River was practically lapping at our front tires! Three more feet and we'd have driven right in!

"There's the taxi!" I shouted.

Over to the right, alongside the river, was the New Abe Taxi! It was stuck axle-deep in the sandy riverbank.

Mom and I jumped out of the car and ran to the taxi.

Grandpa Dan was sitting inside, calmly gazing out at the river.

I leaned in the open passenger window. "Grandpa Dan!"

He turned and gave me a confused look. "What are you doing here, son?"

"We came to get you!"

"Come on out, Dan," Mom said softly. She opened the door for Grandpa Dan. "Everything's fine now. You're going to ride home with us."

"Nobody asked me! I'm fine here!" Grandpa Dan snapped.

I was surprised that he wasn't glad to see us, but Mom just kept talking to him in a real soothing voice.

"Of course, you are. But we came to give you a ride. It'll be fun." She looked over at me. "Won't it be fun, Rio?"

I knew she wanted me to help persuade Grandpa Dan to get out of the taxi. He may be 62 and have memory loss, but he's still strong as an ox.

"Oh, yeah!" I gushed. "It'll be great!"

Grandpa Dan didn't look at all convinced.

"I'm fine right here," he insisted.

"But it's getting dark, Dan," Mom tried again. "Please, let's go." She took his arm, but he shook her off.

"Not now! I need to pick up a customer who wants me to drive him to Joliet!"

I could tell by the frustrated look on Mom's face that she didn't know how to get him out of the taxi.

But, I did!

"Come on with us, Grandpa Dan! It's getting dark and you know what that means!"

He looked at me uncertainly. "Dark?"

I nodded enthusiastically. "And when it gets dark, what's more fun than a forest full of lightning bugs?!"

Grandpa Dan's eyes lit up when he heard those words. "Lightning bugs!"

"Yep!" I continued. "Millions of them!

Putting on a show just for us!"

"Then what are we waiting for?" he suddenly cried out. "Let's hit the road!"

Mom took Grandpa Dan by the arm as I circled around the taxi to join them.

"Lightning bugs will be out in full force any minute now!" Grandpa Dan exclaimed.

"That's right!" Mom agreed. "I can't wait to see them!"

We escorted Grandpa Dan back to our car. I opened the passenger door for him.

He started to get in, but then stopped and looked back. "What about the taxi?"

"We'll get it tomorrow," Mom reassured him.

Grandpa Dan frowned, then suddenly pivoted and started back.

"Dan!" Mom begged in exasperation.

I jumped in his path. He tried to get around me, but I wouldn't let him.

"If we hurry, we'll be able to look out the windows and watch the lightning bugs flash all the way home!" I raved.

Grandpa Dan looked unsure.

"You can sit in front! Mom will be next to you and I'll be right behind you guys!"

He studied my face for a long moment. During that brief time, Grandpa Dan forgot all about the taxi.

All at once, his entire face broke into a big grin. "We better hurry! Lightning bugs will be out in full force any minute now!"

We got Grandpa Dan buckled into the passenger seat. Mom somehow managed to turn the car around and we drove back out to the highway.

This heavily wooded river country is lightning bug heaven! Thousands and thousands of tiny yellow lights twinkled on and off in the growing darkness.

Grandpa Dan stared out the window and grinned from ear to ear.

I sat in the back seat and tried to wipe the tears from my eyes.

-18-
Flop

I knew we'd have a tough time keeping our winning streak alive against the Danville Twisters. Their only loss had been a 2-1 heartbreaker to the Matrix. The Twisters were only one game out of first place, just like the Lightning Bugs. If they beat us, and we somehow beat the Matrix in our final game of the season, the Twisters would be league champs.

Danville was a very good soccer team, but they were even better at acting than at playing soccer! We found that out in the first minute of the match.

Alton accidentally passed the ball into open space near midfield. I turned and sped after it. Out of the corner of my eye, I saw Savanna running unguarded near the center of the penalty area.

The Twisters midfielder ran alongside me stride for stride. But I knew I could beat him to the ball. He bumped into me, but not enough to knock me off-balance. However, he sprawled onto the ground like I'd tripped him!

The referee's whistle stopped play. Danville was awarded a direct free kick.

A minute later, the exact same thing

happened to Mitchie when he accidentally got tangled up with a Twister defender. The defender fell to the ground and Danville got another free kick.

It seemed like every time we got close to the Twisters players, they'd flop on the grass like fish out of water, moaning and groaning in pain.

When Cary was whistled for supposedly knocking down the Twisters striker in the penalty area, Danville was awarded a penalty kick.

Everyone backed away to watch as the striker set the ball down twelve yards from the goal line. Quincy positioned himself in the middle of the goal, ready to dive in either direction.

"Block it, Q!" I yelled.

The striker took a step and drilled the ball at the right corner. Quincy dove, arms fully stretched out, and caught it!

Q maintained possession as he hit the ground. But the referee signaled a goal! Quincy's gloved hands – and the ball – had landed over the goal line! That was the only score in the first half.

As the Lightning Bugs walked to the sideline, I could tell that my teammates were just as frustrated with all the flopping as I was.

"He ran into me and then he fell!" Cary complained.

"I didn't even touch that girl!" Dawson

muttered.

"If they're going to keep flopping, then we should, too!" yelled Fulton.

"Yeah!" several others shouted.

Even a couple of the parents came over to put in their two cents worth.

"It's not a fair fight, Coach! You need to do something!" Fulton's dad urged.

Grandpa Dan hadn't said a word the entire first half. He'd just stood there on the sideline with his arms folded, gazing out at the field.

"At least, talk to the ref about it!" Fulton's dad demanded.

Grandpa Dan didn't respond. I couldn't tell if he understood, or even heard, what everyone was complaining about.

A couple more parents joined the discussion. Everyone within earshot could hear them complaining about the flopping – and blaming our coach for not doing anything!

Mom stood off to the side. By the way she was biting her lip, I knew she was having a real hard time keeping from ripping into those loud-mouthed parents.

"We don't flop," Grandpa Dan said in a quiet voice.

When Grandpa Dan spoke, all the adults and kids spun around toward him.

"What?! That's all Danville's doing!" Fulton's dad protested. "And they're winning, in case you didn't notice!"

"I say, do it right back to 'em!" Sterling's mom joined in.

"Flopping ruins soccer," Grandpa Dan's voice was calm, but firm. "We don't flop."

"It's not fair to our kids!" Fulton's dad yelled. "How do you expect them to have a chance to win?!"

I don't know who elected Fulton's dad leader of this revolt. He needed a cork in his mouth real bad!

"Fulton, you go ahead and play the same way Danville is," said Fulton's dad.

"You too, Sterling!" added Sterling's mom. "What's fair is fair!"

Fulton and Sterling looked at their parents, then at Grandpa Dan. They weren't sure what to do.

I was getting angrier and angrier at the way those parents were openly defying our coach. I knew Mom was, too. She started to step forward.

"Flopping is cheating!" I blurted out. "We don't have to cheat to win!"

Fulton's dad turned to me. "Nobody's saying to cheat, Rio. You guys just need to give the Twisters some of their own medicine."

I desperately wanted to tell him to go jump in a lake, but before I could, Grandpa Dan interrupted.

"Say! Did I ever tell you kids about the time a ghost tapped me on the shoulder?"

Everyone stared at Grandpa Dan, wondering what he was talking about. Mom and I traded nervous looks.

"It was the middle of night. I was out like a log. That's when I dreamed that someone's index finger reached out and tapped me right on my shoulder!"

The kids were looking at Grandpa Dan with wide eyes. The parents exchanged concerned glances.

"I turned the lights on and– "

"Get your hands in here!" I quickly jumped to my feet and stuck out my right hand.

None of the players moved.

Grandpa Dan continued, "Nothing was there!"

"Let's go, Bugs!" Savanna ordered as she stood beside me.

To my relief, the kids all got up and huddled around us.

"If we can't beat them without flopping, then we don't deserve to win!" I looked around at all the faces in the huddle. I wanted them to know that I wasn't joking.

"Like Grandpa Dan said – no flopping!" Savanna's voice made it clear she wasn't joking either.

Heads began nodding in agreement, first a few, then almost everyone.

"Got it, Fulton? Sterling?" Savanna's question wasn't really a question. It was more like a command.

Fulton and Sterling slowly nodded.

"One, two, three!" I shouted.

"Hubba-hubba!" everyone yelled, and we dashed onto the field for the second half.

I took my position as center midfielder and looked over at our sideline. My heart sank.

Although Grandpa Dan was too far away for me to hear anything, it looked like he was still telling that ghost story. Mom linked her arm with his, listening and nodding her head.

The other parents were grouped to the side, glancing back at Grandpa Dan disapprovingly. I could tell they were talking about him.

The Twisters jogged to their positions. As I stood there, looking from the Twisters to our sideline and back again, I felt like I was fighting two battles at once.

I tried to understand why Danville played the way they did. How could anyone think soccer's fun when the ref blows the whistle and stops play every minute?

But the Twisters flopped even more in the second half! Only this time it didn't work out so well for them.

That's because the Lightning Bugs stopped getting frustrated and complaining about it. We got mad and played harder!

Sterling was called for tripping in the penalty area. This time, when the Twisters striker drilled the shot toward the left goalpost, Quincy snagged it. He took two steps and booted the ball toward midfield.

A Danville winger moved over to gather it in, but I leaped up in front of her and headed the ball into their territory.

Mitchie beat a back defender to the ball, then faked left and quickly fired a shot at the near post. I thought for sure it was going in, but the Danville goalkeeper stuck out his leg at the last moment and deflected the ball back onto the field.

Before the back defender could clear the ball away from the goal, Savanna came flying through the air out of nowhere. Her diving header went straight into the net!

On the Twisters' next possession, the ref's whistle blew again. This time, Alton was called for tripping a Danville forward just outside the penalty area.

Cary, Sterling, Alton, and I formed a wall between our goal and the spot where the ref placed the ball for the direct free kick.

We all protected ourselves as much as we could. It's never fun getting smacked by a shot at such close range.

The Danville striker took a step forward and blasted the shot at us. The speeding ball hit Cary right in the stomach. He gasped and fell over backwards!

I looked down at him. "You okay?!"

Cary nodded, rubbing his stomach.

Players from both teams pounced on the loose ball. More players quickly joined in. There must have been a dozen or more kids crowded around the ball. Legs kicked furiously, but no one could free the ball from the tightly packed cluster of bodies.

I reached out my hand and pulled Cary up so we could join the action.

A Danville player accidentally kicked Aurora. She cried out in pain and fell in the middle of the circle. Someone else fell over her.

Bodies piled up as players tripped and fell over each other. It happened so fast, the referee didn't blow his whistle. I guess he couldn't tell who did what to whom.

Aurora was still on the ground at the bottom of the pile. Even though she was crying, she managed to free her leg and push the soccer ball out of the cluster and into the clear!

I bolted forward and gathered in the ball, then took off with it toward midfield. The Twisters defenders were still stuck in the pile-up!

I crossed the halfway line. There was no one between me and the goal except the goalkeeper!

"Go, Rio, go!" I heard Savanna's voice from behind.

I dribbled into the penalty area and headed directly at the keeper. I wanted to keep my options open to shoot left or right.

The keeper came out at me to cut off my angle. He was tall and had long spidery arms, just like Quincy. When he spread them out wide, they practically stretched from goalpost to goalpost!

I decided to blast the shot right at him. The ball whizzed right past his left ear! It hit the crossbar and shot back into play!

Before the keeper could spin around, the ball nailed him in the back of the head! It bounced across the goal line into the net!

The next thing I knew I was lying face-first on the grass and Savanna was celebrating on top of me.

"What a shot, Rio!"

I smiled giddily as I got to my feet. "And I didn't flop! You totaled me!"

As we trotted back for the next kickoff, I looked to the sideline, hoping to see Grandpa Dan celebrating my goal. What I saw nearly killed me.

A Danville police officer was escorting Grandpa Dan and Mom to the parking lot!

-19-
Dead Bugs

Even though I played the remainder of the game against the Danville Twisters, it was like I was sleepwalking. I was too worried about Grandpa Dan to do much of anything on the field.

Fortunately, the rest of the Lightning Bugs held the fort. Quincy stopped everything that came his way, and Savanna scored on a direct free kick in the game's final minute. The Bugs escaped with a 3-1 victory.

After the match, I sprinted straight to the parking lot. I didn't see a police car parked anywhere.

Instead, I spotted Mom and Grandpa Dan sitting in our car!

"Hi, guys!" I jumped in the backseat. "We won! Did you see us?"

"Yes!" Mom answered. "Dan and I were both thrilled! Weren't we, Dan?"

"My brother Pike lives around here somewhere," Grandpa Dan spoke to no one in particular.

"What did the policeman want?" I asked Mom.

Mom shook her head at me, signaling that I

shouldn't bring that up.

"Policeman?" Grandpa Dan frowned as he looked back at me. "What policeman?"

"I don't know," I mumbled. It didn't feel like we'd won anymore.

I'm sure it was one of those know-it-all parents who called the police. I don't see what the big crime is about someone talking about ghosts at a soccer match. Abraham Lincoln's wife talked about ghosts all the time and she lived in the White House!

The Central Illinois Soccer League website updated the standings the next day.

Springfield Matrix	*7-0*
New Abe Lightning Bugs	*6-1*
Danville Twisters	*5-2*
Bloomington Fire	*4-3*
Normal Cardinals	*4-4*
Peoria Pride	*3-4*
Decatur Dynamite	*2-5*
Macomb Zips	*1-6*
Champaign Comets	*0-7*

It was all coming down to the last week of the season! The winner of our game with the Matrix would be crowned Central Illinois League champs!

For us Lightning Bugs, it was going to be the game of the century! I just wished Grandpa Dan was still going to be there to coach.

But it had been decided that Fulton's dad would coach the final game. I didn't really like the way he had spoken to Grandpa Dan over in Danville, but I'm just a kid so I didn't have a say.

I found Grandpa Dan and Pike out back in the garden. They were both digging in the dirt – Grandpa Dan pulling weeds and Pike looking for a bone.

"Hey, Grandpa Dan! Our last soccer match is Saturday!"

He looked up from his labors and grinned. "You don't say!"

"You're coming, aren't you?"

"I wouldn't miss it for the world! Who's playing?"

"Lightning Bugs and Matrix! It's for first place!"

"Sounds like a good one, son!"

I nodded in agreement. He seemed like the old Grandpa Dan the way he was talking to me right now. I almost forgot there was something wrong with him.

"Which one of those teams are you on?" he

asked. As much as I wished he was pretending, I knew Grandpa Dan honestly didn't know.

"Lightning Bugs," I answered softly, forcing a smile.

"Say, did I ever tell you about how the old town of Abe burned down when it was hit by lightning?"

I'd heard Grandpa Dan tell about the big fire plenty of times. I knew how much he enjoyed telling it.

"What happened, Grandpa Dan?" I asked.

"The lightning bolt hit the firehouse, of all places!"

"Really?"

He nodded excitedly. "Once that burned, everything else went with it!"

"Wow!"

"That's why they had to build New Abe!"

"I always wondered about that," I said. I flipped my soccer ball up into the air. "Want to play defense, Pike?"

Pike barked happily and slobbered all over my face.

Grandpa Dan reached out and scratched Pike's fur. "Why'd you name him Pike?"

A lump formed in my throat, making it hard to talk. "He's named after someone who died fighting in a war."

"You don't say! That's a good reason!"

I nodded and smiled. Even though Grandpa Dan didn't remember much anymore, I loved him more than ever!

I hadn't seen Troy Niles in almost a month, not since the end of May when school let out for summer.

That's why I was kind of surprised when I spotted him riding his bike down the street toward my house. On either side of him were the twins who had taken my place on the Matrix.

I didn't really feel like saying anything to them, so I just kind of looked up and nodded my head as they passed.

Unfortunately, they hit the slowed down. Troy gave me a friendly wave. "Hey, Rio, how's it going?"

I knew better than to trust him, so I just nodded again.

"I gotta admit, your Mosquitoes—" he grinned at his friends. "I mean, Lightning Bugs, surprised me. You guys had a pretty decent season," he added. "Should be an awesome game Saturday!"

I'd had enough of his phony talk. "Look, Troy, what do you want?"

"I don't want anything," he sounded hurt.

"Do I, guys?"

The two oversized twins shook their big blockheads.

"Just the opposite, Rio. I have something for you!"

I figured he meant something like a punch in the gut.

"Take a guess!" Troy dangled a see-through plastic bag in his hand. It had something in it, but I couldn't tell what it was.

I shrugged. "Some of your dad's leftover soybeans?"

"Lightning bugs! I caught them just for you!"

Troy had a huge smile on his face, but it wasn't a friendly smile.

I took a step closer, looking. He was right. The bag was filled with at least a hundred lightning bugs – dead ones!

"Look at his face, guys!" Troy shrieked with laughter.

I shuddered and backed away. "You need counseling, Troy. You're disturbed."

Troy opened the bag and dumped the dead bugs onto the street.

"That's what the Matrix are gonna do to your team of little insects!"

He put his heel on top of the pile and started

smashing the lightning bugs into the pavement. His buddies whooped with laughter as they watched him do it.

"Look at him, guys!" Troy snarled. "Poor little Fido's about to cry!"

I could feel something boiling inside me. Something beyond my control. It boiled up and up, ready to explode.

"Woof-woof!" Troy barked and laughed loudly.

I knew it was three against one, but I didn't care! I shot forward to make Troy stop barking. Before I could reach him, Troy knocked me back with a powerful stiff-arm. I tripped and fell awkwardly.

Pain shot through my left side as my elbow and ribs scraped across the curb.

The three boys laughed even louder.

"If I was you, Fido, I wouldn't show up at the game," Troy taunted. "Unless you want to get hurt even worse!"

I could hear them barking and laughing as they rode away. But I didn't watch them.

I was staring at the pile of smashed up lightning bugs in the middle of the street…

And thinking about my great-great-great-great grandfather Charlie Planck…

And Fido Lincoln.

-20-
The Matrix

News of the Lightning Bugs' six game winning streak had spread all over town. It seemed like half the folks of New Abe were at Lincoln Park on Saturday for our final match. The soccer field was lined two-deep with spectators.

As I took my position for the opening kickoff, I could feel the nerves in my stomach start to churn. This was the biggest game of my life.

The Springfield Matrix lined up for the kickoff wearing slick purple and black uniforms. They were the only team in the league that had the players' names on the back of their jerseys.

Troy Niles stood in the center circle. The twins – his blockhead buddies – were positioned on either side of him.

I tried not to look at them. I didn't want to psych myself out thinking about the Matrix's two year unbeaten streak.

So, I looked for Mom and Grandpa Dan. I knew Pike wouldn't be there. We can't ever take Pike to the games because he would run onto the field and try to play defense.

I saw them sitting in canvas folding chairs at the far corner of the field. It looked like Mom was holding Grandpa Dan's hand and talking to him. I wondered what Grandpa Dan thought about all this excitement.

I waved to them, but they didn't see me.

Fulton's dad didn't change the Bugs' starting lineup. I guess he figured, since we'd won six games in a row, our former coach must have been doing something right.

Savanna and Mitchie took their positions near the half-way line. Alton and Aurora flanked me on the wings, and the defenders – Cary and Sterling – spread out in front of Quincy.

Fulton and Dawson always sub in for Alton and Aurora in the first half, and for Cary and Sterling in the second. Nobody ever subbed in for Savanna, Mitchie, and me. We've been on the field for every minute of every game – as has Quincy, since he joined the team.

I could hear Troy and his teammates joking and laughing, but I kept my eyes on the ground in front of me. I thought I heard one of them bark, but I wasn't sure because the hundreds of people on the sidelines were making so much noise.

The referee blew her whistle and I looked up to see Troy push the ball to one of the other forwards. Immediately, the Matrix came at us like an immense purple and black wave.

The ball was passed back to Troy, and I

moved forward to defend him. He dribbled straight at me, so I tried to hold my ground and block him. He side-passed to a winger, then took off running at full-speed past me.

I turned quickly to try to stay with Troy, but one of the Matrix blockhead forwards stepped into my path. He lowered his shoulder and drove it into my chest. I flew backwards, landing on my sore ribs and elbow.

I looked up to see Troy take a return pass from the winger. He faked Sterling with a step over, then drilled a shot just inside the right goalpost. It all happened so fast, Quincy's desperation dive to block the shot was too late.

Less than thirty seconds had elapsed, and the Matrix had a 1-0 advantage!

I checked my elbow. The gauze bandage Mom had wrapped around my arm looked like it had some fresh blood seeping into it.

There was no time to do anything about it because Mitchie passed his kickoff to me. I brought the ball forward two steps, then delivered a pass to Alton on the left flank.

As the action moved in that direction, someone smashed into me from behind and I fell face-first onto the turf. I tried to get up, but the attacker literally ran right over me. His foot planted between my shoulder blades.

"Get outta my way, Fido!"

I looked up as Troy's other blockhead buddy stepped off me and ran downfield. The referee was following the ball, and hadn't seen what happened to me.

A third Matrix player flattened me a short time later. Again, the referee missed it. Although Troy wasn't the one hitting me, I knew he was the mastermind of their violent and completely illegal strategy.

Fulton's dad must have missed it, too. As I got back up a fourth time, he called out, "Stay on your feet, Rio! You can't help the team when you're on the ground!"

I wanted to yell at him to open his eyes, but the Matrix were lining up for a corner kick. Troy set the ball on the corner arc, then bent a high arcing shot toward the goal.

I dashed back and knocked the ball out of bounds before the Matrix forwards could get to it.

Fulton and Dawson ran onto the field to sub in.

Alton and Aurora started off, but Fulton shook his head, "You stay in, Alton! Rio and Aurora are out!"

I couldn't believe it – I was being subbed out!

Fulton's dad clapped his hands as we

reached the sideline. "Good hustle, Aurora! Rio, get your head in the game!"

"But–"

"You look like you didn't come to play!" Fulton's dad barked.

I wanted to defend myself, but I remembered how I felt when Fulton's dad and the other parents had disrespected Grandpa Dan at the last game. I didn't want to be like them.

"Yes, sir…" I answered quietly.

Being forced to stand and watch the game from the sideline was way worse than getting knocked down by a Matrix player every thirty seconds. I felt totally helpless and frustrated. And it got worse by the minute.

Especially when I saw what was happening on the field. Fulton didn't know how to play center mid. He wasn't much of a dribbler, had zero field awareness, and didn't even think of trying to set up Savanna or Mitchie for a shot.

Troy, meanwhile, scored twice more to put the Matrix up by three.

Finally, with two minutes left in the first half, Fulton's dad finally turned to us.

"Aurora, go in for Sterling."

Aurora adjusted her headband and dashed onto the field. Fulton's dad folded his arms across his chest and turned back to watch the game.

I couldn't believe it! Aurora's a very sweet girl, but she's the last person who can turn this game around!

I couldn't control myself. "What about me?"

"You can start the second half," Fulton's dad snapped. "If you think you're ready to play."

Ready to play? I'd never been more ready to play a game in my life!

At least I'd be well rested for the second half. Three goals was a lot to make up against a team as good as the Matrix, but maybe the Bugs can pull off a miracle.

With seconds left in the half, Troy burst through our defenders a final time and blasted the ball past Quincy to make it 4-0.

A second half miracle seemed even more impossible now.

The Lightning Bugs trudged to the sideline. They looked completely defeated.

Savanna grabbed her water bottle and came over to me. "Are you hurt?"

She looked at my bloody elbow, but I just shook my head.

Mitchie plunked down in the grass next to me. "What happened, dude? We need you out there!"

Fulton's dad cleared his throat and shared his words of coaching wisdom. "You guys need to be more aggressive out there. Don't let that Niles boy run around totally unguarded. And we have to get a lot more shots in the second half!"

Nobody paid much attention to his useless advice. Not even his son.

I could tell that Quincy was down on himself for giving up four goals. He kept yanking up blades of grass and mumbling something about Newton's laws.

I scooted over and gave him a slap on the back. "Forget the first half, Q! Just shut 'em out the rest of the way and the offense will do the rest!"

I didn't really believe it, but I knew we had zero chance if the Matrix kept scoring goals.

"Okay, kids! Get out there and… go get 'em!" Fulton's dad clapped his hands enthusiastically and sent the starting lineup back onto the field.

I could hear moans and groans from several players. It was obvious that our replacement coach's attempt to get the team fired up for the second half was a complete failure.

I knew something had to be done right away, or the second half would be a complete massacre – along with our hopes for the league title!

"Huddle up!" I called out as the Lightning

Bugs spread out across the field.

Everyone just kept trudging onto the field.

"I said, huddle up!"

My teammates froze. Even I was surprised at the sudden power of my voice.

Savanna and Mitchie were the first to rejoin me. The others soon followed. We formed a circle right on the field.

I could tell by the defeated looks on my teammates' faces that they were expecting the first half trouncing to continue – and maybe even get worse – in the second half.

"Look, guys… The game's not over." I knew that sounded just as lame as Fulton's dad, but I'm a kid! I had no idea what to say to turn things around.

But Savanna did! "Remember what Grandpa Dan always told us…" She thumped her fist against her chest. "Put your heart into everything you do—"

"And you'll be rewarded!" Mitchie and I were the only ones to finish her sentence.

Savanna nodded at Mitchie and me. Then she turned to the others. "I can't hear you, Bugs!"

She reached up to her ears and took off her sound processors. Then she started grinning.

"Put your heart into everything you do–" Savanna began.

I looked around at all my teammates. I could see a spark being lit!

"And you'll be rewarded!" ten voices shouted together.

"What?!" Savanna urged.

"You'll be rewarded!" This time it was deafening.

Just like that, the Lightning Bugs came back to life!

"I smell cooked goose!" Aurora grinned.

"Matrix goose!" Cary added.

"Stack hands!" Mitchie yelled.

I could literally feel a burst of energy surging through the stack of Lightning Bugs hands.

Dawson finished it off. "One, two, three!"

"Hubba-hubba!" we all yelled, louder than ever.

-21-
A Miracle

I don't know if the Matrix could sense our renewed energy, but they very quickly felt its effect!

On our first possession of the second half, Mitchie and Savanna executed a perfect wall pass. He dished it to her, then, as he broke free, she passed it right back. Mitchie took the pass in full-stride and dribbled toward the goal.

Cooper Sandwich, the Matrix all-star goalkeeper, confidently waited for the shot. He had three shutouts in a row and was planning on getting number four today.

Mitchie faked a kick to the near post. Cooper went for the fake! The back post was wide open!

Unfortunately, Mitchie's foot must have gotten too far under the ball. His point blank shot flew straight up in the air!

Players from both teams looked up and scrambled for position as Mitchie's rocket headed into space, then began its descent.

One of the twin blockhead forwards was in front of me, preventing me from getting closer to the falling missile. I tried to go around him, but he wouldn't let me.

The ball was dropping fast! Another second and—

I grabbed onto the forward's massive shoulders and launched myself vertically. I shot up high, above everyone's head.

I looked up and… the soccer ball smacked against my forehead! It happened so fast, I didn't have time to aim.

I was still airborne, so I had a perfect view as the ball sailed toward the goal! The shot was high, but it looked like it would go under the crossbar!

The keeper leaped up as high as he could. His gloved hand stretched higher than I thought possible!

The ball struck his hand and deflected up. I watched it hit the crossbar and bounce back down into the goal!

The next second, I was back on the ground, buried under a pile of celebrating Lightning Bugs. My forehead still stung where the ball hit… but it was a good sting!

The Matrix players looked stunned as they lined up for the next kickoff.

Troy sneered at me. "Lucky, that's all!"

I pretended not to hear him. In a way, I was glad Troy was being Troy. That kind of put-down always makes me play even harder.

Moments after the Matrix kickoff, I smothered Troy as he tried to advance the ball across the half-way line. He passed it to a winger, then took off sprinting. I knew what was coming next!

Instead of letting that blockhead forward drive his shoulder into me again, I darted around him and sped after Troy. When the Matrix winger passed the ball back to Troy, I cut in front of him and stole it away.

Out of the corner of my eye, I saw Savanna streaking down the field. I needed to pass the ball out in front of her, but knew that would be difficult as fast as she runs.

I locked my ankle and kicked the center of the ball with the laces of my cleats. The long pass rose up high and sailed far downfield. It landed out in front of Savanna!

She gathered it in without breaking stride! A defender slid in front of her to try to take the ball away, but Savanna jumped over him and kept dribbling toward the goal!

The Matrix goalkeeper crouched low, his arms spread wide.

Savanna swung her powerful right leg at the ball.

Cooper Sandwich leaned left, toward the

near post.

Savanna's right foot swung over the ball. As the keeper dove and grabbed air, Savanna calmly side-kicked the ball with her left foot into the wide-open goal!

Just like that, we'd cut the Matrix lead in half! Maybe we *could* pull off a miracle!

For the next ten minutes, the Lightning Bugs continued on the attack. However, the Matrix defense stiffened.

There was a reason they hadn't been beaten in two years. Not only were the Matrix an extremely confident and talented group of soccer players, they played with what seemed like an unbreakable will to win.

But their confidence was shaken to its core when the miracle occurred.

With only two minutes left in the match and still trailing 4-2, the Lightning Bugs unleashed a furious offensive assault. We flooded the goal area with seven attackers – everyone except Quincy.

It was pure rapid-fire action as Savanna, Mitchie, and I bombarded the goal with close-in shots. If we scored quickly, there might still be enough time to get one more goal and tie the game!

But Cooper Sandwich met every challenge. He looked superhuman as he jumped, twirled, and dove in front of the goal. Cooper blocked every single one of our shots!

Finally, with just over a minute to play, I drilled one at the left goalpost. Cooper kicked his leg out and deflected my shot with his shin!

Luckily, the ball bounced right toward Aurora! She was standing by herself in front of the right goalpost! No one was within five feet of her!

Aurora stepped forward to kick the ball into the open net, but her feet got tangled. She stumbled and fell flat on her face across the goal line as the ball rolled past her!

Alton beat the Matrix defender to the ball near the corner flag. He spun around the defender and sent a flick pass right to Savanna. She used the side of her shoe to one-time a rocket toward the goal.

Again, the keeper stopped it – this time with his forearm!

The ball flew right at Fulton. He had a wide-open look! But he hurried it. His shot missed wide left and flew out of bounds!

I couldn't believe it… None of us could… The Matrix players started celebrating their victory as the keeper retrieved the ball.

There was less than a minute to play. Cooper Sandwich trotted slowly back onto the field. You could tell he was in no big hurry since the clock continued to run.

Players from both teams scrambled back toward midfield to receive Cooper's goal kick.

Aurora was still getting to her feet at the goal line after blowing her big chance to finally score a goal and help the team. I couldn't imagine how awful she must have felt.

The keeper rolled the ball out onto the grass in front of him. He hesitated, using up more clock, before starting forward to kick it.

He didn't see Aurora behind him!

When Aurora spotted the soccer ball rolling freely in front of the goal, her eyes grew big. She darted around the surprised keeper just as he swung his leg!

Aurora stole the ball and quickly circled to try to get off a shot! The furious keeper charged at her, but Aurora used her little body to shield him from the ball.

Before he knew what happened, Aurora ducked under his arm. The unguarded goal was right in front of her – just five yards away!

Cooper lunged in desperation as Aurora swung her leg.

Her foot almost missed the ball, but she got enough of it to send it rolling slowly toward the goal. From where I was standing, it didn't look like the ball had enough speed to cross the goal line!

Cooper dove – his outstretched fingers reached to stop the shot!

Instead, his fingers grazed the ball and pushed it farther! All the keeper could do was lay there and watch as Aurora's shot slowly trickled over the goal line!

Half of the fans on the sidelines started cheering like crazy. The other half stood there in stunned silence.

Mitchie and Savanna were the first to Aurora. They picked her up and held her aloft as all the Bugs swarmed excitedly. Aurora grinned as she took off her rainbow headband and thrust it up at the sky.

The Matrix players looked shocked. Their lead had been cut to 4-3! They hadn't been in a match this close in forever!

Unfortunately, the Matrix still had one huge advantage. There was less than half a minute to play! If they kept possession of the ball and killed the clock, 4-3 would be the final score!

And the Springfield Matrix would once again be Central Illinois League champs!

"Bugs! Remember..." I yelled as we hurriedly lined up for the kickoff. "Put your heart into everything you do–"

"–and you'll be rewarded!" everyone

thundered.

I'm sure the match's final minute was unlike anything soccer fans of Sangamon County had ever seen. If anybody was filming it, they'll be showing it over and over far into the future.

With only seconds left in the match, Troy received the kickoff pass and started dribbling backwards to kill the clock.

I started toward him. But before I could get there, a blur suddenly came out of nowhere!

I watched in total amazement as Troy was literally spun around in a 360!

It happened so fast, the Matrix players didn't have time to react! They just stood there like statues as Savanna stole the ball from Troy!

She dribbled right between the stunned defenders and raced toward the goal like there were rockets on the bottom of her shoes!

All of a sudden, Cooper Sandwich didn't look so confident. In fact, he looked like he wanted to hide.

Savanna bore down on him and blasted a shot! The ball hit the keeper right in the ribs!

Cooper grunted in pain, but was able to wrap his arms around the ball. Matrix players and fans started celebrating.

The incredible force of Savanna's shot drove the keeper backwards. Cooper lost his balance and did a backwards somersault into the goal. He ended up tangled in the goal net – the ball lying there next to him!

Goal!

I heard the final whistle as we all mobbed Savanna!

The game ended in a 4-4 tie!

-22-
Shoot-out

Except the match *wasn't* over! Central Illinois League teams have a penalty shoot-out when matches end in a tie! Quincy and I had researched that, too.

A shoot-out is when one player from each team takes a penalty kick. Whoever scores, wins. If both players score – or both miss – two more players take a turn.

The Lightning Bugs hadn't ever played a game that ended with a shoot-out, so there was some confusion on the sideline as we clustered around Fulton's dad.

"Savanna should kick!" I told him.

"Yep! She'll nail the PK!" Mitchie agreed.

"Well, let's see…" Fulton's dad was trying to figure out a plan. "Quincy, you'll be the goalkeeper."

I don't know why he said that, since everyone already knew it. I guess he was nervous.

"And, uh…" he paused and looked over at his son. "Okay, Savanna, you take the shot."

All the Bugs pounded Savanna's back and gave her high fives. Then we flooded back onto the field to watch the shoot-out!

Troy already was at the penalty mark waiting to kick first. Quincy took his position midway between the goalposts. All the other players on both teams stood near the center circle.

I cupped my hands to my mouth, "Piece of cake, Q!"

My teammates shouted their support to Quincy. Matrix players tried to drown us out by cheering loudly for Troy. Troy grinned and pumped his fist in the air.

The referee placed the ball on the penalty mark in front of the goal. The grin on Troy's face immediately disappeared. In its place – a look of total focus and determination.

Quincy rocked side to side on the balls of his feet. His arms were extended, his eyes locked on the ball sitting at the penalty mark.

The crowd stilled as Troy took a deep breath and stepped toward the ball. He booted a laser at the right goalpost.

Quincy dove, but his back foot slipped. He fell awkwardly as Troy's shot zipped untouched into the net!

Troy turned around and bowed to his cheering teammates in the center circle. "Piece of cake!" he smirked as he looked in my direction.

Quincy limped out of the goal and collapsed in the grass, rubbing his ankle. Cooper Sandwich moved into position between the posts to await Savanna's kick.

The referee again placed the soccer ball on the penalty mark.

We all cheered as Savanna trotted forward to take her turn, but the Matrix players chanted even louder.

"Miss it! Miss it! Miss it!"

Savanna stepped back and readied herself. The crowd didn't quiet down like they had for Troy's kick. The Matrix players yelled even louder.

"Miss it! Miss it! Miss it!"

Grandpa Dan would never have allowed the Lightning Bugs to taunt an opponent like that. He thought that kind of behavior was poor sportsmanship.

Mr. Niles just stood there on the Matrix sideline. He sucked on a soybean and said nothing.

From midfield, I looked at Savanna's back and wished as hard as I could that she'd score.

"Miss it! Miss it! Miss it!" all the Matrix players screamed, louder and louder.

Wait! The sound processors weren't on Savanna's ears! She was holding them in her hands!

"Miss it! Miss it! Miss it!"

Hah! She couldn't hear anything the Matrix

players were screaming!

Savanna took a deep breath and stepped toward the ball. Before the keeper could even react, she sent a shot screaming into the back of the net!

The game was still tied! Two different shooters would try again!

One of the blockhead Matrix forwards headed for the penalty mark.

I turned to see who Fulton's dad would pick next. I figured it would be either Mitchie or me.

But our coach wasn't on the sideline! I didn't see him anywhere around!

"Look!" Mitchie pointed toward the goal.

Quincy's dad and Fulton's dad were helping our injured keeper to his feet. Quincy's right knee was bent to keep his foot off the ground.

Once they moved Quincy to the sideline, the referee blew her whistle.

"Need a new keeper, Coach!" she called.

I didn't hear what Fulton's dad said because I was already sprinting for the goal. I'd played goalkeeper for the Bugs in the first game of the season and I'd do it again in the last one!

"Another dead Lightning Bug!" the Matrix forward sneered as I ran past.

I stopped just in front of the goal line, exactly between the goalposts, and looked out at the kicker.

The referee placed the ball on the penalty mark. The entire crowd cheered wildly as the Matrix forward backed up two steps.

He was looking toward the goalpost to my right. That could mean two things – he was going to shoot to my right, or he was trying to fake me out by looking right and was going to shoot to my left!

It was useless to try to read his mind. I wasn't sure he even had one! I had to quickly do what Quincy's does in goal… hyper-focus!

The crowd was still yelling like crazy, but now it sounded farther and farther away. The only thing I was focused on was the soccer ball sitting motionless on the grass at the penalty mark.

The forward's right foot suddenly slammed against the ball! I dove to my right, extended my arm, and easily deflected the shot away from the goal!

I could hear my teammates cheering, but when I stood up, I looked over at Grandpa Dan.

Mom was jumping up and down and yelling her head off. But Grandpa Dan just stared out at the field. He had kind of a blank look on his face. I guess I was hoping for something impossible.

Mitchie was up next. If he could somehow score on Cooper, the Lightning Bugs would be league champs!

The Matrix keeper moved into position between the posts. He looked relieved that someone other than Savanna was taking the PK.

Mitchie stepped back to line up his shot. The Matrix players resumed their chant, now even louder.

"Miss it! Miss it! Miss it!"

I could tell that the taunting bothered Mitchie. As if to end it, he hurriedly charged forward and kicked the ball.

Cooper Sandwich jumped up, but he didn't have to. The ball sailed high above his head and over the crossbar!

Mitchie's shoulders slumped.

"Almost!" I gave Mitchie a fist bump as I returned to the goal. The shoot-out was going to round three!

This time, Mr. Niles sent Wayne Crete to the penalty mark. I'd played soccer with Wayne plenty of times, and knew he had a big bend on his powerful left-footed shots.

The referee placed the ball on the mark. Wayne stepped back to line up his shot.

I had no idea which way he would kick it. He might boot it right at me, then count on the bend to spin it out of my reach!

All the players and fans were shouting at the

top of their lungs. Through the roar, I thought I heard Quincy's voice.

I turned and saw him standing on one leg with his hands cupped to his mouth. He was yelling something about Newton's laws of motion!

I turned my focus to the ball waiting on the grass. I crouched slightly and extended my arms, elbows bent. The bloody gauze bandage hung loose, partly unraveled.

Wayne stepped forward and struck the ball squarely with the laces of his left soccer boot

The ball sped toward the goalpost to my right, but I forced myself not to overreact. I was counting on Wayne's vicious bend to bring the ball back right to where I was standing!

Except that it wasn't bending! It was heading straight for the net just inches inside the post!

I dove in desperation, knowing I was too late!

A sharp pain cut through the nail of my right forefinger. As I crash-landed against the post, I looked up – the spinning ball hit the crossbar and bounced over the goal!

I immediately jumped up and raced back to my teammates at the center circle. I didn't even stop to look at my finger. I didn't care whether the knuckle was busted or the nail ripped clean off!

All the Lightning Bugs fans were going completely nuts! Even the Matrix fans were looking pretty amazed by the back and forth drama!

As the Bugs congratulated me, Savanna grabbed my arm.

"Finish it off, Rio!"

I'd totally forgotten that I'd be the next kicker for the Bugs! Instead of getting a moment to catch my breath, I dashed right back to the penalty mark.

"Go, Rio, go!" My teammates were cheering so loudly, I couldn't even hear the Matrix players!

The referee placed the ball on the grass, then moved aside so I could take the penalty kick. Cooper Sandwich stared out at me, rocking slowly back and forth, poised to block my shot.

I didn't know where to kick it – right, left, high, low. As a center mid, penalty kicks weren't something I did much.

Suddenly, I heard a new taunt swelling up behind me. Not *Miss it!...* but a sound that was far more disturbing – the crazed barking of a dozen rabid Springfield Matrix dogs!

The ref signaled to me to take the kick, but I just stood there. I couldn't block out the awful noise! The barking drowned out everything! It filled my ears, then my entire head! It even seemed to invade my vision.

I looked down at the ball, but all I saw was a dog – a dead dog! The insane barking grew louder and louder! I couldn't stop thinking about Fido Lincoln!

Again, the ref motioned for me to kick. But, I couldn't do it! I was frozen, frozen in fear! Maybe Alton or Sterling could take my place!

Then, the strangest thing happened. As I looked down again at the ball, Fido looked up at me – and smiled! He smiled right at me!

It was like he was forgiving me!

I glanced down at my hands – they were clean! I knew I'd never see blood on them again!

And all the barking… it just sounded like a bunch of stupid, annoying kids.

As I stepped toward the ball, all the crowd noise faded away. My mind just kind of went blank. It was like my body knew what to do even if my mind didn't!

The laces of my right shoe slammed against the ball. I watched as if in slow motion as the ball sailed to the right! The keeper dove to block it!

But Cooper couldn't reach it! He couldn't reach it because the shot was too wide! The ball hit the right goalpost and ricocheted left along the goal line! It sailed right over Cooper's horizontal body!

I watched as the soccer ball banged off the left goalpost and bounced into the back of the net!

I just stood there, staring in disbelief at the ball in the goal.

A deafening cheer rang in my ears. I spun around and was immediately buried under a sweaty pile of screaming Lightning Bugs.

It was the best feeling ever!

When I finally got to my feet, Savanna ran at me with her arms open wide.

"League champs!" she rejoiced. She squeezed me so hard, I think she bent a couple of my ribs.

"Yeah! Not bad for a bunch of ultra rejects!" I laughed.

Someone grabbed my arm. I turned and saw the last person on Earth I wanted to see – Troy Niles. He was probably ready to vaporize me since he couldn't beat us fair and square on the field.

"Great game." The way the words came out of his mouth, I could tell it wasn't the easiest thing for Troy to say.

He held out his fist for me to bump, but I didn't move. I was waiting for him to call me what he always calls me.

"Rio…" Troy said. If that wasn't shocking enough, he smiled. And not a mean smile like usual. It was friendly.

Although my great-great-great-great grandfather would always be the one who killed Fido Lincoln, I had a feeling that Troy would never remind me of that again.

Even if he or anyone else ever did, I knew it wouldn't bother me – because I didn't feel like a dog killer anymore.

I was done feeling bad about being related to Charlie Planck. After all, there wasn't anything I could do to change the awful thing he did.

I bumped Troy's fist, then saw Quincy limping toward me, a big grin on his face.

"Way to use Newton's Laws, Rio!" he shouted.

"Yeah," I laughed and gave him a high five. "Everything I know about physics – and playing goalie – I learned from you!"

Then I turned and sped off to find Grandpa Dan and Mom.

"The Bugs did it! Rio scored the winner!" Mom tried to celebrate with Grandpa Dan, but he just sat there. His blank expression didn't change.

"Wow, Rio! What an incredible finish!" Mom gave me a big hug.

"Thanks, Mom!"

I don't know which made me feel better – winning the championship or seeing how happy it made Mom.

"Grandpa Dan! Look, it's Rio! Our soccer champion!"

Grandpa Dan nodded mechanically, then looked down at his feet.

I knelt beside him. "Did you see the game, Grandpa Dan?!"

He looked up at me like he had no idea what I was talking about.

"The Lightning Bugs – your team. We won the championship!" I told him excitedly.

He still showed no sign of understanding. His face turned back down toward the ground.

I looked over at Mom. She just shook her head sadly.

But I wasn't giving up. I knew exactly what to say to him.

"We cooked their goose, Grandpa Dan!"

I thought I saw a tiny spark of memory flash in Grandpa Dan's eyes.

"We cooked their goose but good! Didn't we, Grandpa Dan?... Didn't we?!"

Grandpa Dan's head slowly came upward. He had a look on his face like he'd just remembered something long forgotten.

"We sure did, son!" he suddenly blurted out. "We cooked their goose but good!"

His eyes were filled with a light that had been missing for too long. I held up my hand and

Grandpa Dan gave me a high five.

"It was a real nail-biter, wasn't it, Grandpa Dan?" I continued, trying to use every old saying I could think of. "I bet you were on pins and needles!"

"I was on pins and needles the whole time!" A big grin spread across Grandpa Dan's face, same as always.

"It's all because of what you taught us, Grandpa Dan! Put your heart into everything you do–"

"And you'll be rewarded!" Grandpa Dan shouted. Then he got up out of the canvas chair and started dancing a little jig.

"*Mijo*!" Mom put her arm around me as we watched Grandpa Dan celebrate. "He still remembers those crazy sayings, all those idioms!"

I grinned and nodded.

"Ready to get the show on the road, Grandpa Dan?" I called to him.

"Let's hit it, son!"

I grabbed the two canvas chairs and Mom took Grandpa Dan by the hand.

"Where we headed?" he asked cheerfully.

Mom looked over at me to answer.

"We're going home, Grandpa Dan!" I said brightly. "It'll be more fun than a forest full of lightning bugs!"

"Hubba-hubba!" Grandpa Dan sang out happily. He jumped up high, his free hand punching at the sky.

"Hubba-hubba!" laughed Mom.

Deep down I knew that Grandpa Dan's disease wasn't going to get better. But for right now, I felt so happy I almost jumped straight out of my skin!

"Hubba-hubba!" I yelled, louder than I'd ever yelled before.

www.ingramcontent.com/pod-product-compliance
Lightning Source LLC
LaVergne TN
LVHW090943080826
845145LV00003B/874

* 9 7 8 0 9 6 4 4 1 0 1 1 4 *